SELECTED POEMS

C. DAY LEWIS

SELECTED POEMS

HARPER & ROW, PUBLISHERS

NEW YORK

AND EVANSTON

This selection is dedicated to Albert and Barbara Gelpi

Contents

[v]

Foreword

Casting back over my verse of the last forty years is an uncomfortable experience, and makes any selection from it seem an arbitrary one. Evidently I wrote all those poems; but the successive I's who wrote them are mostly strangers to me now. The ageing poet is rebuked by his youth—by its happily spendthrift nature: so many concepts unrealised, so many images botched, so many poems that never grew to wholeness; but the prodigality, the impatience, the wide-openness to joy and pain, the brave confidence of his earlier selves—these are what he envies now. It is all said in my poem, 'The Rebuke.'

I can see certain themes, certain obsessive states of mind, recurring throughout my verse: admiration for the heroic, a sense of life's transience, the riddle of identity. I suppose it is inevitable that poems embodying such themes should commend themselves most to me. But which are the 'best' of these, I have little idea. Technical tests prove nothing but technical success or failure: they are no criterion of poetic truth, the ideal Emily Dickinson envisaged when she said, 'Art is a house which tries to be haunted.'

It is easy to see the influences: Yeats, for example, the English Metaphysicals, Hopkins, Auden, Hardy, Meredith, Frost. Mediators, I would prefer to call them, rather than influences; for they are men whose work helped me to approach and open up new fields for my own verse, made me aware of the potentiality in subjects I had previously ignored, and showed me a way in to them. Such was the benign effect of these poets. If an influence proved bad for me in the longer run, it was through my over-susceptibility to other men's ways of using words, so that I found myself imitating instead of deriving.

These poets taught me how to write poetry, and how difficult it is to write a good poem. And I learnt from them that poetry is not—except in a very limited sense—a form of self-expression. Who on earth supposes that the pearl expresses the oyster?

It has been said, rightly, that the poet is a parasite—not only on the work of other poets, but on society. He feeds wherever he can find sustenance for his work; and when one host fails, he drops off and seeks another. The social-conscience verse of the Thirties (though in fact only a small proportion of our poems were directly political) arose from a situation in which the plight of society and the private life cast light on each other for the poet, and cross-fertilised each other. That situation changed; we turned to other areas and interpretations of experience—I myself to more 'personal' subjects. Yet, however intimate the experience, it is always, for me writing the poem, out there, a piece of the Other.

I think, in my earlier verse as in my later, I always wished to be lucid. Through whatever changes of style, I have wanted to make sense out of the chaotic jumble of my own ideas, feelings, impressions. If I can discover for myself, through a poem, the meaning of a given experience, something will also be communicated to the reader. I can seldom achieve such lucidity except through strict form. The limiting and liberating nature of poetic form, as I see it, is stated in the second stanza of my poem, 'On Not Saying Everything.'

> Unwritten poems loom as if
> They'd cover the whole of earthly life.
> But each one, growing, learns to trim its
> Impulse and meaning to the limits

Roughed out by me, then modified
In its own truth's expanding light.
A poem, settling to its form,
Finds there's no jailer, but a norm
Of conduct, and a fitting sphere
Which stops it wandering everywhere.

                                    C. D. L.

For I had been a modern moth and hurled
Myself on many a flaming world,
To find its globe was glass.
In you alone
I met the naked light, by you became
Veteran of a flame
That burns away all but the warrior bone.
And I shall know, if time should falsify
This star the company of my night,
Mine is the heron's flight
Which makes a solitude of any sky.

From

TRANSITIONAL POEM

(1929)

That afternoon we lay

That afternoon we lay on Lillington Common
The land wallowed around us in the sunlight;
But finding all things my strenuous sense included
Ciphers new-copied by the indefinite sunlight,
I fell once more under the shadow of my Sphinx.
The aimlessness of buttercup and beetle
So pestered me, I would have cried surrender
To the fossil certitudes of Tom, Dick, and Harry,
Had I known how or believed that such a surrender
Could fashion aught but a dead Sphinx from the live Sphinx.
Later we lit a fire, and the hedge of darkness—
Garnished with not a nightingale nor a glow-worm—
Sprang up like the beanstalk by which our Jack aspired once.
Then, though each star seemed little as a glow-worm
Perched on Leviathan's flank, and equally terrible
My tenure of this plateau that sloped on all sides
Into annihilation—yet was I lord of
Something: for, seeing the fall of a burnt-out faggot
Make all the night sag down, I became lord of
Light's interplay—stoker of an old parable.

Desire is a witch

Desire is a witch
And runs against the clock.
It can unstitch
The decent hem
Where space tacks on to time:
It can unlock
Pandora's privacies.

It puffs in these
Top-gallants of the mind,
And away I stand
On the elemental gale
Into an ocean
That the liar Lucian
Had never dared retail.

When my love leans with all
Her shining breast and shoulder,
I know she is older
Than Ararat the hill,
And yet more young
Than the first daffodil
That ever shews a spring.

When her eyes delay
On me, so deep are they
Tunnelled by love, although
You poured Atlantic
In this one and Pacific

In the other, I know
They would not overflow.

Desire clicks back
Like cuckoo into clock;
Leaves me to explain
Eyes that a tear will drown
And a body where youth
Nor age will long remain
To implicate the truth.

It seems that we must call
Anything truth whose well
Is deep enough;
For the essential
Philosopher-stone, desire,
Needs no other proof
Than its own fire.

When nature plays

When nature plays hedge-schoolmaster,
Shakes out the gaudy map of summer
And shows me charabanc, rose, barley-ear
And every bright-winged hummer,

He only would require of me
To be the sponge of natural laws
And learn no more of that cosmography
Than passes through the pores.

Why must I then unleash my brain
To sweat after some revelation
Behind the rose, heedless if truth maintain
On the rose-bloom her station?

When bullying April bruised mine eyes
With sleet-bound appetites and crude
Experiments of green, I still was wise
And kissed the blossoming rod.

Now summer brings what April took,
Riding with fanfares from the south,
And I should be no Solomon to look
My Sheba in the mouth.

Charabancs shout along the lane
And summer gales bay in the wood
No less superbly because I can't explain
What I have understood.

Let logic analyse the hive,
Wisdom's content to have the honey:
So I'll go bite the crust of things and thrive
While hedgerows still are sunny.

With me, my lover makes

With me, my lover makes
  The clock assert its chime:
But when she goes, she takes
  The mainspring out of time.

Yet this time-wrecking charm
  Were better than love dead
And its hollow alarum
  Hammered out on lead.

Why should I fear that Time
  Will superannuate
These workmen of my rhyme—
  Love, despair and hate?

Fleeing the herd, I came
  To a graveyard on a hill,
And felt its mould proclaim
  The bone gregarious still.

Boredoms and agonies
  Work out the rhythm of bone—
No peace till creature his
  Creator has outgrown.

Passion dies from the heart
  But to infect the marrow;
Holds dream and act apart
  Till the man discard his narrow

Sapience and folly
   Here, where the graves slumber
In a green melancholy
   Of overblown summer.

From

FROM FEATHERS TO IRON

(1931)

Suppose that we

Suppose that we, tomorrow or the next day,
Came to an end—in storm the shafting broken,
Or a mistaken signal, the flange lifting—
Would that be premature, a text for sorrow?

Say what endurance gives or death denies us.
Love's proved in its creation, not eternity:
Like leaf or linnet the true heart's affection
Is born, dies later, asks no reassurance.

Over dark wood rises one dawn felicitous,
Bright through awakened shadows fall her crystal
Cadenzas, and once for all the wood is quickened.
So our joys visit us, and it suffices.

Nor fear we now to live who in the valley
Of the shadow of life have found a causeway;
For love restores the nerve and love is under
Our feet resilient. Shall we be weary?

Some say we walk out of Time altogether
This way into a region where the primrose
Shows an immortal dew, sun at meridian
Stands up for ever and in scent the lime tree.

This is a land which later we may tell of.
Here-now we know, what death cannot diminish
Needs no replenishing; yet certain are, though
Dying were well enough, to live is better.

Passion has grown full man by his first birthday.
Running across the bean-fields in a south wind,
Fording the river mouth to feel the tide-race—
Child's play that was, though proof of our possessions.

Now our research is done, measured the shadow,
The plains mapped out, the hills a natural boundary.
Such and such is our country. There remains to
Plough up the meadowland, reclaim the marshes.

Beauty's end is in sight

Beauty's end is in sight,
Terminus where all feather joys alight.
Wings that flew lightly
Fold and are iron. We see
The thin end of mortality.

We must a little part,
And sprouting seed crack our cemented heart.
Who would get an heir
Initial loss must bear:
A part of each will be elsewhere.

What life may now decide
Is past the clutch of caution, the range of pride.
Speaking from the snow
The crocus lets me know
That there is life to come, and go.

Waning is now the sensual eye

Waning is now the sensual eye
Allowed no flaw upon the skin
And burnt away wrinkle and feature,
Fed with pure spirit from within.

Nesciently that vision works.
Just so the pure night-eye, the moon,
Labours, a monumental mason,
To gloss over a world of stone.

Look how she marbled heath and terrace,
Effacing boundary and date.
She took the sky; earth was below her
A shining shell, a featherweight.

No more may pupil love bend over
A plane theorem, black and white.
The interlocking hours revolve,
The globe goes lumbering into light.

Admiral earth breaks out his colours
Bright at the forepeak of the day;
Hills in their hosts escort the sun
And valleys welcome him their way.

Shadow takes depth and shape turns solid:
Far-ranging, the creative eye
Sees arable, marsh, enclosed and common,
Assents to multiplicity.

Do not expect again

Do not expect again a phœnix hour,
The triple-towered sky, the dove complaining,
Sudden the rain of gold and heart's first ease
Tranced under trees by the eldritch light of sundown.

By a blazed trail our joy will be returning:
One burning hour throws light a thousand ways,
And hot blood stays into familiar gestures.
The best years wait, the body's plenitude.

Consider then, my lover, this is the end
Of the lark's ascending, the hawk's unearthly hover:
Spring season is over soon and first heatwave;
Grave-browed with cloud ponders the huge horizon.

Draw up the dew. Swell with pacific violence.
Take shape in silence. Grow as the clouds grew.
Beautiful brood the cornlands, and you are heavy;
Leafy the boughs—they also hide big fruit.

Beauty breaks ground

Beauty breaks ground, oh, in strange places.
Seen after cloudburst down the bone-dry watercourses,
In Texas a great gusher, a grain-
Elevator in the Ukraine plain;
To a new generation turns new faces.

Here too fountains will soon be flowing.
Empty the hills where love was lying late, was playing,
Shall spring to life: we shall find there
Milk and honey for love's heir,
Shadow from sun also, deep ground for growing.

My love is a good land. The stranger
Entering here was sure he need prospect no further.
Acres that were the eyes' delight
Now feed another appetite.
What formed her first for seed, for crop must change her.

This is my land. I've overheard it
Making a promise out of clay. All is recorded—
Early green, drought, ripeness, rainfall,
Our village fears and festivals,
When the first tractor came and how we cheered it.

And as the wind whose note will deepen
In the upgrowing tree, who runs for miles to open
His throat above the wood, my song
With that increasing life grew strong,
And will have there a finished form to sleep in.

From

THE MAGNETIC MOUNTAIN

(1933)

But Two there are

But Two there are, shadow us everywhere
And will not let us be till we are dead,
Hardening the bones, keeping the spirit spare,
Original in water, earth and air,
Our bitter cordial, our daily bread.

Turning over old follies in ante-room,
For first-born waiting or for late reprieve,
Watching the safety-valve, the slackening loom,
Abed, abroad, at every turn and tomb
A shadow starts, a hand is on your sleeve.

O you, my comrade, now or tomorrow flayed
Alive, crazed by the nibbling nerve; my friend
Whom hate has cornered or whom love betrayed,
By hunger sapped, trapped by a stealthy side,
Brave for so long but whimpering in the end:

Such are the temporal princes, fear and pain,
Whose borders march with the ice-fields of death,
And from that servitude escape there's none
Till in the grave we set up house alone
And buy our liberty with our last breath.

Nearing again the legendary isle

Nearing again the legendary isle
Where sirens sang and mariners were skinned,
We wonder now what was there to beguile
That such stout fellows left their bones behind.

Those chorus-girls are surely past their prime,
Voices grow shrill and paint is wearing thin,
Lips that sealed up the sense from gnawing time
Now beg the favour with a graveyard grin.

We have no flesh to spare and they can't bite,
Hunger and sweat have stripped us to the bone;
A skeleton crew we toil upon the tide
And mock the theme-song meant to lure us on:

No need to stop the ears, avert the eyes
From purple rhetoric of evening skies.

Live you by love confined

Live you by love confined,
There is no nearer nearness;
Break not his light bounds,
The stars' and seas' harness:
There is nothing beyond,
We have found the land's end.
We'll take no mortal wound
Who felt him in the furnace,
Drowned in his fierceness,
By his midsummer browned:
Nor ever lose awareness
Of nearness and farness
Who've stood at earth's heart careless
Of suns and storms around,
Who have leant on the hedge of the wind,
On the last ledge of darkness.

We are where love has come
To live: he is that river
Which flows and is the same;
He is not the famous deceiver
Nor early-flowering dream.
Content you. Be at home
In me. There's but one room
Of all the house you may never
Share, deny or enter.
There, as a candle's beam
Stands firm and will not waver
Spire-straight in a close chamber,

As though in shadowy cave a
Stalagmite of flame,
The integral spirit climbs
The dark in light for ever.

From

A TIME TO DANCE

(1935)

Learning to Talk

See this small one, tiptoe on
The green foothills of the years,
Views a younger world than yours;
When you go down, he'll be the tall one.

Dawn's dew is on his tongue—
No word for what's behind the sky,
Naming all that meets the eye,
Pleased with sunlight over a lawn.

Hear his laughter. He can't contain
The exquisite moment overflowing.
Limbs leaping, woodpecker flying
Are for him and not hereafter.

Tongue trips, recovers, triumphs,
Turning all ways to express
What the forward eye can guess—
That time is his and earth young.

We are growing too like trees
To give the rising wind a voice:
Eagles shall build upon our verse,
Our winged seeds are tomorrow's sowing.

Yes, we learn to speak for all
Whose hearts here are not at home,
All who march to a better time
And breed the world for which they burn.

Though we fall once, though we often,
Though we fall to rise not again,
From our horizon sons begin;
When we go down, they will be tall ones.

The Conflict

I sang as one
Who on a tilting deck sings
To keep men's courage up, though the wave hangs
That shall cut off their sun.

As storm-cocks sing,
Flinging their natural answer in the wind's teeth,
And care not if it is waste of breath
Or birth-carol of spring.

As ocean-flyer clings
To height, to the last drop of spirit driving on
While yet ahead is land to be won
And work for wings.

Singing I was at peace,
Above the clouds, outside the ring:
For sorrow finds a swift release in song
And pride its poise.

Yet living here,
As one between two massing powers I live
Whom neutrality cannot save
Nor occupation cheer.

None such shall be left alive:
The innocent wing is soon shot down,
And private stars fade in the blood-red dawn
Where two worlds strive.

The red advance of life
Contracts pride, calls out the common blood,
Beats song into a single blade,
Makes a depth-charge of grief.

Move then with new desires,
For where we used to build and love
Is no man's land, and only ghosts can live
Between two fires.

The Ecstatic

Lark, skylark, spilling your rubbed and round
Pebbles of sound in air's still lake,
Whose widening circles fill the noon; yet none
Is known so small beside the sun:

Be strong your fervent soaring, your skyward air!
Tremble there, a nerve of song!
Float up there where voice and wing are one,
A singing star, a note of light!

Buoyed, embayed in heaven's noon-wide reaches—
For soon light's tide will turn— Oh stay!
Cease not till day streams to the west, then down
That estuary drop down to peace.

Two Songs

I've heard them lilting at loom and belting,
Lasses lilting before dawn of day:
But now they are silent, not gamesome and gallant—
The flowers of the town are rotting away.

There was laughter and loving in the lanes at evening;
Handsome were the boys then, and girls were gay.
But lost in Flanders by medalled commanders
The lads of the village are vanished away.

Cursed be the promise that takes our men from us—
All will be champion if you choose to obey:
They fight against hunger but still it is stronger—
The prime of our land grows cold as the clay.

The women are weary, once lilted so merry,
Waiting to marry for a year and a day:
From wooing and winning, from owning or earning
The flowers of the town are all turned away.

    Come, live with me and be my love,
    And we will all the pleasures prove
    Of peace and plenty, bed and board,
    That chance employment may afford.

    I'll handle dainties on the docks
    And thou shalt read of summer frocks:
    At evening by the sour canals
    We'll hope to hear some madrigals.

Care on the maiden brow shall put
A wreath of wrinkles, and thy foot
Be shod with pain: not silken dress
But toil shall tire thy loveliness.

Hunger shall make thy modest zone
And cheat fond death of all but bone—
If these delights thy mind may move,
Then live with me and be my love.

A Carol

Oh hush thee, my baby,
Thy cradle's in pawn:
No blankets to cover thee
Cold and forlorn.
The stars in the bright sky
Look down and are dumb
At the heir of the ages
Asleep in a slum.

The hooters are blowing,
No heed let him take;
When baby is hungry
'Tis best not to wake.
Thy mother is crying,
Thy dad's on the dole:
Two shillings a week is
The price of a soul.

From

OVERTURES TO DEATH

(1938)

Newsreel

Enter the dream-house, brothers and sisters, leaving
Your debts asleep, your history at the door:
This is the home for heroes, and this loving
Darkness a fur you can afford.

Fish in their tank electrically heated
Nose without envy the glass wall: for them
Clerk, spy, nurse, killer, prince, the great and the defeated,
Move in a mute day-dream.

Bathed in this common source, you gape incurious
At what your active hours have willed—
Sleep-walking on that silver wall, the furious
Sick shapes and pregnant fancies of your world.

There is the mayor opening the oyster season:
A society wedding: the autumn hats look swell:
An old crocks' race, and a politician
In fishing-waders to prove that all is well.

Oh, look at the warplanes! Screaming hysteric treble
In the long power-dive, like gannets they fall steep.
But what are they to trouble—
These silver shadows to trouble your watery, womb-deep sleep?

See the big guns, rising, groping, erected
To plant death in your world's soft womb.
Fire-bud, smoke-blossom, iron seed projected—
Are these exotics? They will grow nearer home:

Grow nearer home—and out of the dream-house stumbling
One night into a strangling air and the flung
Rags of children and thunder of stone niagaras tumbling,
You'll know you slept too long.

Overtures to Death

The sun came out in April

The sun came out in April,
The hawthorn in May:
We thought the year, like other years,
Would go the Christmas way.

In June we picked the clover,
And sea-shells in July:
There was no silence at the door,
No word from the sky.

A hand came out of August
And flicked his life away:
We had not time to bargain, mope,
Moralize, or pray.

Where he had been, was only
An effigy on a bed
To ask us searching questions or
Hear what we'd left unsaid.

Only that stained parchment
Set out what he had been—
A face we might have learned better,
But now must read unseen.

Thus he resigned his interest
And claims, all in a breath,
Leaving us the long office work
And winding-up of death:

The ordinary anguish,
The stairs, the awkward turn,
The bearers' hats like black mushrooms
Placed upon the lawn.

As a migrant remembers
The sting and warmth of home,
As the fruit bears out the blossom's word,
We remember him.

He loved the sun in April,
The hawthorn in May:
Our tree will not light up for him
Another Christmas Day.

It is not you I fear

It is not you I fear, but the humiliations
You mercifully use to deaden grief—
The downward graph of natural joys,
Imagination's slump, the blunted ear.

I hate this cold and politic self-defence
Of hardening arteries and nerves
Grown dull with time-serving. I see that the heart lives
By self-betrayal, by circumspection is killed.

That boy, whose glance makes heaven open and edges
Each dawning pain with gold, must learn to disbelieve:
The wildfire lust of the eyes will gutter down
To age's dim recalcitrance.

Have we not seen how quick this young girl's thoughts,
Wayward and burning as a charm of goldfinches
Alarmed from thistle-tops, turn into
Spite or a cupboard love or clipped routine?

Nearing the watershed and the difficult passes,
Man wraps up closer against the chill
In his familiar habits; and at the top
Pauses, seeing your kingdom like a net beneath him spread.

Some climbed to this momentous peak of the world
And facing the horizon—that notorious pure woman
Who lures to cheat the last embrace,
Hurled themselves down upon an easier doom.

One the rare air made dizzy renounced
Earth, and the avalanche took him at his word:
One wooed perfection—he's bedded deep in the glacier, perfect
And null, the prince and image of despair.

The best, neither hoarding nor squandering
The radiant flesh and the receptive
Spirit, stepped on together in the rhythm of comrades who
Have found a route on earth's true reckoning based.

They have not known the false humility,
The shamming-dead of the senses beneath your hunter's hand;
But life's green standards they've advanced
To the limit of your salt unyielding zone.

The Nabara*

> *They preferred, because of the rudeness of their heart, to die rather than*
> *to surrender.*

PHASE ONE

Freedom is more than a word, more than the base coinage
Of statesmen, the tyrant's dishonoured cheque, or the dreamer's
> mad
Inflated currency. She is mortal, we know, and made
In the image of simple men who have no taste for carnage
But sooner kill and are killed than see that image betrayed.
Mortal she is, yet rising always refreshed from her ashes:
She is bound to earth, yet she flies as high as a passage bird
To home wherever man's heart with seasonal warmth is stirred:
Innocent is her touch as the dawn's, but still it unleashes
The ravisher shades of envy. Freedom is more than a word.

I see man's heart two-edged, keen both for death and creation.
As a sculptor rejoices, stabbing and mutilating the stone
Into a shapelier life, and the two joys make one—
So man is wrought in his hour of agony and elation
To efface the flesh to reveal the crying need of his bone.
Burning the issue was beyond their mild forecasting
For those I tell of—men used to the tolerable joy and hurt
Of simple lives: they coveted never an epic part;
But history's hand was upon them and hewed an everlasting
Image of freedom out of their rude and stubborn heart.

* The episode upon which this poem is based is related in G. L. Steer's
The Tree of Gernika.

The year, Nineteen-thirty-seven: month, March: the men, de-
                                                                scendants
Of those Iberian fathers, the inquiring ones who would go
Wherever the sea-ways led: a pacific people, slow
To feel ambition, loving their laws and their independence—
Men of the Basque country, the Mar Cantabrico.
Fishermen, with no guile outside their craft, they had weathered
Often the sierra-ranked Biscayan surges, the wet
Fog of the Newfoundland Banks: they were fond of *pelota:* they
                                                                met
No game beyond their skill as they swept the sea together,
Until the morning they found the leviathan in their net.

Government trawlers *Nabara, Guipuzkoa, Bizkaya,*
Donostia, escorting across blockaded seas
Galdames with her cargo of nickel and refugees
From Bayonne to Bilbao, while the crest of war curled higher
Inland over the glacial valleys, the ancient ease.
On the morning of March the fifth, a chill North-Wester fanned
                                                                them,
Fogging the glassy waves: what uncharted doom lay low
There in the fog athwart their course, they could not know:
Stout were the armed trawlers, redoubtable those who manned
                                                                them—
Men of the Basque country, the Mar Cantabrico.

Slowly they nosed ahead, while under the chill North-Wester
Nervous the sea crawled and twitched like the skin of a beast
That dreams of the chase, the kill, the blood-beslavered feast:
They too, the light-hearted sailors, dreamed of a fine fiesta,
Flags and their children waving, when they won home from the
                                                                east.

[43]

Vague as images seen in a misted glass or the vision
Of crystal-gazer, the ships huddled, receded, neared,
Threading the weird fog-maze that coiled their funnels and bleared
Day's eye. They were glad of the fog till *Galdames* lost position—
Their convoy, precious in life and metal—and disappeared.

But still they held their course, the confident ear-ringed captains,
Unerring towards the landfall, nor guessed how the land lay,
How the guardian fog was a guide to lead them all astray.
For now, at a wink, the mist rolled up like the film that curtains
A saurian's eye; and into the glare of an evil day
Bizkaya, Guipuzkoa, Nabara, and the little
Donostia stepped at intervals; and sighted, alas,
Blocking the sea and sky a mountain they might not pass,
An isle thrown up volcanic and smoking, a giant in metal
Astride their path—the rebel cruiser, *Canarias.*

A ship of ten thousand tons she was, a heavyweight fighter
To the cocky bantam trawlers: and under her armament
Of eight- and four-inch guns there followed obedient
Towards Pasajes a prize just seized, an Estonian freighter
Laden with arms the exporters of death to Spain had sent.
A hush, the first qualm of conflict, falls on the cruiser's burnished
Turrets, the trawlers' grimy decks: fiercer the lime-
Light falls, and out of the solemn ring the late mists climb,
And ship to ship the antagonists gaze at each other astonished
Across the quaking gulf of the sea for a moment's time.

The trawlers' men had no chance or wish to elude the fated
Encounter. Freedom to these was natural pride that runs
Hot as the blood, their climate and heritage, dearer than sons.

[44]

Bizkaya, Guipuzkoa, knowing themselves outweighted,
Drew closer to draw first blood with their pairs of four-inch guns.
Aboard Canarias the German gun-layers stationed
Brisk at their intricate batteries—guns and men both trained
To a hair in accuracy, aimed at a pitiless end—
Fired, and the smoke rolled forth over the unimpassioned
Face of a day where nothing certain but death remained.

PHASE TWO

The sound of the first salvo skimmed the ocean and thumped
Cape Machichaco's granite ribs: it rebounded where
The salt-sprayed trees grow tough from wrestling the wind: it
                                                          jumped
From isle to rocky isle: it was heard by women while
They walked to shrine or market, a warning they must fear.
But, beyond their alarm, as
Though that sound were also a signal for fate to strip
Luck's last green shoot from the falling stock of the Basques,
                                                          Galdames
Emerged out of the mist that lingered to the west
Under the reeking muzzles of the rebel battleship:

Which instantly threw five shells over her funnel, and threw
Her hundred women and children into a slaughter-yard panic
On the deck they imagined smoking with worse than the foggy
                                                          dew,
So that Galdames rolled as they slipped, clawed, trampled, reeled
Away from the gape of the cruiser's guns. A spasm galvanic,
Fear's chemistry, shocked the women's bodies, a moment before
Huddled like sheep in a mist, inert as bales of rag,

[45]

A mere deck-cargo; but more
Than furies now, for they stormed Galdames' bridge and swarmed
Over her captain and forced him to run up the white flag.

Signalling the Estonian, 'Heave-to,' Canarias steamed
Leisurely over to make sure of this other prize:
Over-leisurely was her reckoning—she never dreamed
The Estonian in that pause could be snatched from her shark-shape
                                                            jaws
By ships of minnow size.
Meanwhile Nabara and Guipuzkoa, not reluctant
For closer grips while their guns and crews were still entire,
Thrust forward: twice Guipuzkoa with a deadly jolt was rocked,
                                                            and
The sea spat up in geysers of boiling foam, as the cruiser's
Heavier guns boxed them in a torrid zone of fire.

And now the little Donostia who lay with her 75's
Dumb in the offing—her weapons against that leviathan
Impotent as pen-knives—
Witnessed a bold manœuvre, a move of genius, never
In naval history told. She saw Bizkaya run
Ahead of her consorts, a berserk atom of steel, audacious,
Her signal-flags soon to flutter like banderillas, straight
Towards the Estonian speeding, a young bull over the spacious
And foam-distraught arena, till the sides of the freight-ship screen
                                                            her
From Canarias that will see the point of her charge too late.

'Who are you and where are you going?' the flags of Bizkaya ques-
                                                            tioned.
'Carrying arms and forced to go to Pasajes,' replied

The Estonian. 'Follow me to harbour.' 'Cannot, am threatened.'
Bizkaya's last word—'Turn at once!'—and she points her peremp-
tory guns
Against the freighter's mountainous flanks that blankly hide
This fluttering language and flaunt of signal insolence
From the eyes of *Canarias.* At last the rebels can see
That the two ships' talk meant a practical joke at their expense:
They see the Estonian veering away, to Bermeo steering,
Bizkaya under her lee.

(To the Basques that ship was a tonic, for she carried some million
rounds
Of ammunition: to hearts grown sick with hope deferred
And the drain of their country's wounds
She brought what most they needed in face of the aid evaded
And the cold delay of those to whom freedom was only a word.)*
Owlish upon the water sat the *Carnarias*
Mobbed by those darting trawlers, and her signals blinked in vain
After the freighter, that still she believed too large to pass
Into Bermeo's port—a prize she fondly thought,
When she'd blown the trawlers out of the water, she'd take again.

Brisk at their intricate batteries the German gun-layers go
About death's business, knowing their longer reach must foil
The impetus, break the heart of the government ship each blow
Deliberately they aim, and tiger-striped with flame

---

* Cf. Byron's comments upon 'Non-Intervention' in *The Age of Bronze:*
    Lone, lost, abandoned in their utmost need
    By Christians, unto whom they gave their creed,
    The desolated lands, the ravaged isle,
    The fostered feud encouraged to beguile,
    The aid evaded, and the cold delay
    Prolonged but in the hope to make a prey:—
    These, these shall tell the tale, and Greece can show
    The false friend worse than the infuriate foe.

Is the jungle mirk of the smoke as their guns leap and recoil.
The Newfoundland trawlers feel
A hail and hurricane the like they have never known
In all their deep-sea life: they wince at the squalls of steel
That burst on their open decks, rake them and leave them wrecks,
But still they fight on long into the sunless afternoon.

—Fought on, four guns against the best of the rebel navy,
Until *Guipuzkoa's* crew could stanch the fires no more
That gushed from her gashes and seeped nearer the magazine.
                                                        Heavy
At heart they turned away for the Nervion that day:
Their ship, *Guipuzkoa*, wore
Flame's rose on her heart like a decoration of highest honour
As listing she reeled into Las Arenas; and in a row

On her deck there lay, smoke-palled, that oriflamme's crackling
                                                        banner
Above them, her dead—a quarter of the fishermen who had fought
                                                        her—
Men of the Basque country, the Mar Cantabrico.

PHASE THREE

And now the gallant *Nabara* was left in the ring alone,
The sky hollow around her, the fawning sea at her side:
But the ear-ringed crew in their berets stood to the guns, and cried
A fresh defiance down
The ebb of the afternoon, the battle's darkening tide.
Honour was satisfied long since; they had held and harried
A ship ten times their size; they well could have called it a day.

[48]

But they hoped, if a little longer they kept the cruiser in play,
Galdames with the wealth of life and metal she carried
Might make her getaway.

Canarias, though easily she outpaced and out-gunned her,
Finding this midge could sting
Edged off, and beneath a wedge of smoke steamed in a ring
On the rim of the trawler's range, a circular storm of thunder.
But always Nabara turned her broadside, manœuvring
To keep both guns on the target, scorning safety devices.
Slower now battle's tempo, irregular the beat
Of gunfire in the heart
Of the afternoon, the distempered sky sank to the crisis,
Shell-shocked the sea tossed and hissed in delirious heat.

The battle's tempo slowed, for the cruiser could take her time,
And the guns of Nabara grew
Red-hot, and of fifty-two Basque seamen had been her crew
Many were dead already, the rest filthy with grime
And their comrades' blood, weary with wounds all but a few.
Between two fires they fought, for the sparks that flashing spoke
From the cruiser's thunder-bulk were answered on their own craft
By traitor flames that crawled out of every cranny and rift
Blinding them all with smoke.
At half-past four Nabara was burning fore and aft.

What buoyancy of will
Was theirs to keep her afloat, no vessel now but a sieve—
So jarred and scarred, the rivets starting, no inch of her safe
From the guns of the foe that wrapped her in a cyclone of shrieking
steel!

[49]

Southward the sheltering havens showed clear, the cliffs and the
                                                                surf
Familiar to them from childhood, the shapes of a life still dear:
But dearer still to see
Those shores insured for life from the shadow of tyranny.
Freedom was not on their lips; it was what made them endure,
A steel spring in the yielding flesh, a thirst to be free.

And now from the little *Donostia* that lay with her 75's
Dumb in the offing, they saw *Nabara* painfully lower
A boat, which crawled like a shattered crab slower and slower
Towards them. They cheered the survivors, thankful to save these
                                                                lives
At least. They saw each rower,
As the boat dragged alongside, was wounded—the oars they held
Dripping with blood, a bloody skein reeled out in their wake:
And they swarmed down the rope-ladders to rescue these men so
                                                                weak
From wounds they must be hauled
Aboard like babies. And then they saw they had made a mistake.

For, standing up in the boat,
A man of that grimy boat's-crew hailed them: 'Our officer asks
You give us your bandages and all your water-casks,
Then run for Bermeo. We're going to finish this game of *pelota*.'
Donostia's captain begged them with tears to escape: but the
                                                                Basques
Would play their game to the end.
They took the bandages, and cursing at his delay
They took the casks that might keep the fires on their ship at bay;
And they rowed back to *Nabara*, trailing their blood behind
Over the water, the sunset and crimson ebb of their day.

[50]

For two hours more they fought, while Nabara beneath their feet
Was turned to a heap of smouldering scrap-iron. Once again
The flames they had checked a while broke out. When the forward
gun
Was hit, they turned about
Bringing the after gun to bear. They fought in pain
An the instant knowledge of death: but the waters filling their
riven
Ship could not quench the love that fired them. As each man fell
To the deck, his body took fire as if death made visible
That burning spirit. For two more hours they fought, and at seven
They fired their last shell.

Of her officers all but one were dead. Of her engineers
All but one were dead. Of the fifty-two that had sailed
In her, all were dead but fourteen—and each of these half-killed
With wounds. And the night-dew fell in a hush of ashen tears,
And Nabara's tongue was stilled.
Southward the sheltering havens grew dark, the cliffs and the green
Shallows they knew; where their friends had watched them as
evening wore
To a glowing end, who swore
Nabara must show a white flag now, but saw instead the fourteen
Climb into their matchwood boat and fainting pull for the shore.

Canarias lowered a launch that swept in a greyhound's curve
Pitiless to pursue
And cut them off. But that bloodless and all-but-phantom crew
Still gave no soft concessions to fate: they strung their nerve
For one last fling of defiance, they shipped their oars and threw
Hand-grenades at the launch as it circled about to board them.
But the strength of the hands that had carved them a hold on
history

Failed them at last: the grenades fell short of the enemy,
Who grappled and overpowered them,
While Nabara sank by the stern in the hushed Cantabrian sea.

        *   *   *   *   *

They bore not a charmed life. They went into battle foreseeing
Probable loss, and they lost. The tides of Biscay flow
Over the obstinate bones of many, the winds are sighing
Round prison walls where the rest are doomed like their ship to
                                     rust—
Men of the Basque country, the Mar Cantabrico.
Simple men who asked of their life no mythical splendour,
They loved its familiar ways so well that they preferred
In the rudeness of their heart to die rather than to surrender . . .
Mortal these words and the deed they remember, but cast a seed
Shall flower for an age when freedom is man's creative word.

Freedom was more than a word, more than the base coinage
Of politicians who hiding behind the skirts of peace
They had defiled, gave up that country to rack and carnage:
For whom, indelibly stamped with history's contempt,
Remains but to haunt the blackened shell of their policies.
For these I have told of, freedom was flesh and blood—a mortal
Body, the gun-breech hot to its touch: yet the battle's height
Raised it to love's meridian and held it awhile immortal;
And its light through time still flashes like a star's that has turned
                                     to ashes,
Long after Nabara's passion was quenched in the sea's heart.

Passage from Childhood

His earliest memory, the mood
Fingered and frail as maidenhair,
Was this—a china cup somewhere
In a green, deep wood.
He lives to find again somewhere
That wood, that homely cup; to taste all
Its chill, imagined dews; to dare
The dangerous crystal.

Who can say what misfeatured elf
First led him into that lifelong
Passage of mirrors where, so young,
He saw himself
Balanced as Blondin, more headstrong
Than baby Hercules, rare as a one-
Cent British Guiana, above the wrong
And common run?

He knew the secrecy of squirrels,
The foolish doves' antiphony,
And what wrens fear. He was gun-shy,
Hating all quarrels.
Life was a hostile land to spy,
Full of questions he dared not ask
Lest the answer in mockery
Or worse unmask.

Quick to injustice, quick he grew
This hermit and contorted shell.

Self-pity like a thin rain fell,
Fouling the view:
Then tree-trunks seemed wet roots of hell,
Wren or catkin might turn vicious,
The dandelion clock could tell
Nothing auspicious.

No exile has ever looked so glum
With the pines fretful overhead,
Yet he felt at home in the gothic glade—
More than at home.
You will forgive him that he played
Bumble-puppy on the small mossed lawn
All by himself for hours, afraid
Of being born.

Lying awake one night, he saw
Eternity stretched like a howl of pain:
He was tiny and terrible, a new pin
On a glacier's floor.
Very few they are who have lain
With eternity and lived to tell it:
There's a secret process in his brain
And he cannot sell it.

Now, beyond reach of sense or reason,
His life walks in a glacial sleep
For ever, since he drank that cup
And found it poison.
He's one more ghost, engaged to keep
Eternity's long hours and mewed
Up in live flesh with no escape
From solitude.

From

WORD OVER ALL

(1943)

Departure in the Dark

Nothing so sharply reminds a man he is mortal
As leaving a place
In a winter morning's dark, the air on his face
Unkind as the touch of sweating metal:
Simple goodbyes to children or friends become
A felon's numb
Farewell, and love that was a warm, a meeting place—
Love is the suicide's grave under the nettles.

Gloomed and clemmed as if by an imminent ice-age
Lies the dear world
Of your street-strolling, field-faring. The senses, curled
At the dead end of a shrinking passage,
Care not if close the inveterate hunters creep,
And memories sleep
Like mammoths in lost caves. Drear, extinct is the world,
And has no voice for consolation or presage.

There is always something at such times of the passover,
When the dazed heart
Beats for it knows not what, whether you part
From home or prison, acquaintance or lover—
Something wrong with the time-table, something unreal
In the scrambled meal
And the bag ready packed by the door, as though the heart
Has gone ahead, or is staying here for ever.

No doubt for the Israelites that early morning
It was hard to be sure

If home were prison or prison home: the desire
Going forth meets the desire returning.
This land, that had cut their pride down to the bone
Was now their own
By ancient deeds of sorrow. Beyond, there was nothing sure
But a desert of freedom to quench their fugitive yearnings.

At this blind hour the heart is informed of nature's
Ruling that man
Should be nowhere a more tenacious settler than
Among wry thorns and ruins, yet nurture
A seed of discontent in his ripest ease.
There's a kind of release
And a kind of torment in every goodbye for every man
And will be, even to the last of his dark departures.

O Dreams, O Destinations

1

For infants time is like a humming shell
Heard between sleep and sleep, wherein the shores
Foam-fringed, wind-fluted of the strange earth dwell
And the sea's cavernous hunger faintly roars.
It is the humming pole of summer lanes
Whose sound quivers like heat-haze endlessly
Over the corn, over the poppied plains—
An emanation from the earth or sky.
Faintly they hear, through the womb's lingering haze,
A rumour of that sea to which they are born:
They hear the ringing pole of summer days,
But need not know what hungers for the corn.
They are the lisping rushes in a stream—
Grace-notes of a profound, legato dream.

2

Children look down upon the morning-grey
Tissue of mist that veils a valley's lap:
Their fingers itch to tear it and unwrap
The flags, the roundabouts, the gala day.
They watch the spring rise inexhaustibly—
A breathing thread out of the eddied sand,
Sufficient to their day: but half their mind
Is on the sailed and glittering estuary.
Fondly we wish their mist might never break,
Knowing it hides so much that best were hidden:

We'd chain them by the spring, lest it should broaden
For them into a quicksand and a wreck.
But they slip through our fingers like the source,
Like mist, like time that has flagged out their course.

3

That was the fatal move, the ruination
Of innocence so innocently begun,
When in the lawless orchard of creation
The child left this fruit for that rosier one.
Reaching towards the far thing, we begin it;
Looking beyond, or backward, more and more
We grow unfaithful to the unique minute
Till, from neglect, its features stale and blur.
Fish, bird or beast was never thus unfaithful—
Man only casts the image of his joys
Beyond his senses' reach; and by this fateful
Act, he confirms the ambiguous power of choice.
Innocence made that first choice. It is she
Who weeps, a child chained to the outraged tree.

4

Our youthtime passes down a colonnade
Shafted with alternating light and shade.
All's dark or dazzle there. Half in a dream
Rapturously we move, yet half afraid
Never to wake. That diamond-point, extreme
Brilliance engraved on us a classic theme:
The shaft of darkness had its lustre too,

Rising where earth's concentric mysteries gleam.
Oh youth-charmed hours, that made an avenue
Of fountains playing us on to love's full view,
A cypress walk to some romantic grave—
Waking, how false in outline and in hue
We find the dreams that flickered on our cave:
Only your fire, which cast them, still seems true.

5

All that time there was thunder in the air:
Our nerves branched and flickered with summer lightning.
The taut crab-apple, the pampas quivering, the glare
On the roses seemed irrelevant, or a heightening
At most of the sealed-up hour wherein we awaited
What?—some explosive oracle to abash
The platitudes on the lawn? heaven's delegated
Angel—the golden rod, our burning bush?
No storm broke. Yet in retrospect the rose
Mounting vermilion, fading, glowing again
Like a fire's heart, that breathless inspiration
Of pampas grass, crab-tree's attentive pose
Never were so divinely charged as then—
The veiled Word's flesh, a near annunciation.

6

Symbols of gross experience!—our grief
Flowed, like a sacred river, underground:
Desire bred fierce abstractions on the mind,
Then like an eagle soared beyond belief.
Often we tried our breast against the thorn,

Our paces on the turf: whither we flew,
Why we should agonize, we hardly knew—
Nor what ached in us, asking to be born.
Ennui of youth!—thin air above the clouds,
Vain divination of the sunless stream
Mirror that impotence, till we redeem
Our birthright, and the shadowplay concludes.
Ah, not in dreams, but when our souls engage
With the common mesh and moil, we come of age.

7

Older, we build a road where once our active
Heat threw up mountains and the deep dales veined:
We're glad to gain the limited objective,
Knowing the war we fight in has no end.
The road must needs follow each contour moulded
By that fire in its losing fight with earth:
We march over our past, we may behold it
Dreaming a slave's dream on our bivouac hearth.
Lost the archaic dawn wherein we started,
The appetite for wholeness: now we prize
Half-loaves, half-truths—enough for the half-hearted,
The gleam snatched from corruption satisfies.
Dead youth, forgive us if, all but defeated,
We raise a trophy where your honour lies.

8

But look, the old illusion still returns,
Walking a field-path where the succory burns
Like summer's eye, blue lustre-drops of noon,

And the heart follows it and freshly yearns:
Yearns to the sighing distances beyond
Each height of happiness, the vista drowned
In gold-dust haze, and dreams itself immune
From change and night to which all else is bound.
Love, we have caught perfection for a day
As succory holds a gem of halcyon ray:
Summer burns out, its flower will tarnish soon—
Deathless illusion, that could so relay
The truth of flesh and spirit, sun and clay
Singing for once together all in tune!

9

To travel like a bird, lightly to view
Deserts where stone gods founder in the sand,
Ocean embraced in a white sleep with land;
To escape time, always to start anew.
To settle like a bird, make one devoted
Gesture of permanence upon the spray
Of shaken stars and autumns; in a bay
Beyond the crestfallen surges to have floated.
Each is our wish. Alas, the bird flies blind,
Hooded by a dark sense of destination:
Her weight on the glass calm leaves no impression,
Her home is soon a basketful of wind.
Travellers, we're fabric of the road we go;
We settle, but like feathers on time's flow.

The Assertion

Now, in the face of destruction,
In the face of the woman knifed out of all recognition
By flying glass, the fighter spinning like vertigo
On the axis of the trapped pilot and crowds applauding,
Famine that bores like a death-watch deep below,
Notice of agony splashed on headline and hoarding,
In the face of the infant burned
To death, and the shattered ship's-boat low in the trough—
Oars weakly waving like a beetle overturned—
Now, as never before, when man seems born to hurt
And a whole wincing earth not wide enough
For his ill will, now is the time we assert
To their face that men are love.

For love's no laughing matter,
Never was a free gift, an angel, a fixed equator.
Love's the big boss at whose side for ever slouches
The shadow of the gunman: he's mortar and dynamite;
Antelope, drinking pool, but the tiger too that crouches.
Therefore be wise in the dark hour to admit
The logic of the gunman's trigger,
Embrace the explosive elements, learn the need
Of tiger for antelope and antelope for tiger.
O love, so honest of face, so unjust in action,
Never so dangerous as when denied,
Let your kindness tell us how false we are, your bloody correction
Our purpose and our pride.

Where Are the War Poets?

They who in folly or mere greed
Enslaved religion, markets, laws,
Borrow our language now and bid
Us to speak up in freedom's cause.

It is the logic of our times,
No subject for immortal verse—
That we who lived by honest dreams
Defend the bad against the worse.

Reconciliation

All day beside the shattered tank he'd lain
Like a limp creature hacked out of its shell,
Now shrivelling on the desert's grid,
Now floating above a sharp-set ridge of pain.

There came a roar, like water, in his ear.
The mortal dust was laid. He seemed to be lying
In a cool coffin of stone walls,
While memory slid towards a plunging weir.

The time that was, the time that might have been
Find in this shell of stone a chance to kiss
Before they part eternally:
He feels a world without, a world within

Wrestle like old antagonists, until each is
Balancing each. Then, in a heavenly calm,
The lock gates open, and beyond
Appear the argent, swan-assemblied reaches.

The Rebuke

Down in the lost and April days
What lies we told, what lies we told!
Nakedness seemed the one disgrace,
And there'd be time enough to praise
The truth when we were old.

The irresponsible poets sung
What came into their head:
Time to pick and choose among
The bold profusions of our tongue
When we were dead, when we were dead.

Oh wild the words we uttered then
In woman's ear, in woman's ear,
Believing all we promised when
Each kiss created earth again
And every far was near.

Little we guessed, who spoke the word
Of hope and freedom high
Spontaneously as wind or bird
To crowds like cornfields still or stirred,
It was a lie, a heart-felt lie.

Now the years advance into
A calmer stream, a colder stream,
We doubt the flame that once we knew,
Heroic words sound all untrue
As love-lies in a dream.

Yet fools are the old who won't be taught
Modesty by their youth:
That pandemonium of the heart,
That sensual arrogance did impart
A kind of truth, a kindling truth.

Where are the sparks at random sown,
The spendthrift fire, the holy fire?
Who cares a damn for truth that's grown
Exhausted haggling for its own
And speaks without desire?

From

POEMS 1943–1947

(1948)

The Double Vision

The river this November afternoon
Rests in an equipoise of sun and cloud:
A glooming light, a gleaming darkness shroud
Its passage. All seems tranquil, all in tune.

Image and real are joined like Siamese twins:
Their doubles draw the willows, a brown mare
Drinks her reflection. There's no margin where
Substance leaves off, the illusory begins.

You and I by the river contemplate
Our ideal selves, glossed here, crystal-divined:
We yearn to them, knowing one sigh of wind
Will rub these precious figures from the slate.

It is not of their transience I'm afraid,
But thinking how most human loves protract
Themselves to unreality—the fact
Drained of its virtue by the image it made.

O double vision of the autumnal stream,
Teach me to bear love's fusion or diffusion!
O gems of purest water, pure illusion,
Answer my rays and cluster to a theme!

A Failure

The soil was deep and the field well-sited,
    The seed was sound.
Average luck with the weather, one thought,
    And the crop would abound.

If harrowing were all that is needed for
    Harvest, his field
Had been harrowed enough, God knows, to warrant
    A record yield.

He gazed from a hill in the breezy springtime:
    That field was aflow
With wave upon wave like a sea's green shallows
    Breathing below.

He looked from a gate one summer morning
    When the mists uprolled:
Headland to headland those fortunate acres
    Seemed solid gold.

He stood by the field as the day of harvest
    Dawned. But, oh,
The fruit of a year's work, a lifetime's lore,
    Had ceased to grow.

No wickedest weather could thus have turned,
    As it were overnight,
His field to so wan and weedy a showing:
    Some galloping blight

From earth's metabolism must have sprung
    To ruin all;
Or perhaps his own high hopes had made
    The wizened look tall.

But it's useless to argue the why and wherefore.
    When a crop is so thin,
There's nothing to do but to set the teeth
    And plough it in.

Statuette: Late Minoan

Girl of the musing mouth,
The mild archaic air,
For whom do you subtly smile?
Yield to what power or prayer
Breasts vernally bare?

I seem to be peering at you
Through the wrong end of time
That shrinks to a bright, far image—
Great Mother of earth's prime—
A stature sublime.

So many golden ages
Of sunshine steeped your clay,
So dear did the maker cherish
In you life's fostering ray,
That you warm us today.

Goddess or girl, you are earth.
The smile, the offered breast—
They were the dream of one
Thirsting as I for rest,
As I, unblest.

Emily Brontë

All is the same still. Earth and heaven locked in
A wrestling dream the seasons cannot break:
Shrill the wind tormenting my obdurate thorn trees,
Moss-rose and stone-chat silent in its wake.
Time has not altered here the rhythms I was rocked in,
Creation's throb and ache.

All is yet the same, for mine was a country
Stoic, unregenerate, beyond the power
Of man to mollify or God to disburden—
An ingrown landscape none might long endure
But one who could meet with a passion wilder-wintry
The scalding breath of the moor.

All is yet the same as when I roved the heather
Chained to a demon through the shrieking night,
Took him by the throat while he flailed my sibylline
Assenting breast, and won him to delight.
O truth and pain immortally bound together!
O lamp the storm made bright!

Still on those heights prophetic winds are raving,
Heath and harebell intone a plainsong grief:
'Shrink, soul of man, shrink into your valleys—
Too sharp that agony, that spring too brief!
Love, though your love is but the forged engraving
Of hope on a stricken leaf!'

Is there one whom blizzards warm and rains enkindle
And the bitterest furnace could no more refine?

Anywhere one too proud for consolation,
Burning for pure freedom so that he will pine,
Yes, to the grave without her? Let him mingle
His barren dust with mine.

But is there one who faithfully has planted
His seed of light in the heart's deepest scar?
When the night is darkest, when the wind is keenest,
He, he shall find upclimbing from afar
Over his pain my chaste, my disenchanted
And death-rebuking star.

Birthday Poem for Thomas Hardy

Is it birthday weather for you, dear soul?
Is it fine your way,
With tall moon-daisies alight, and the mole
Busy, and elegant hares at play
By meadow paths where once you would stroll
In the flush of day?

I fancy the beasts and flowers there beguiled
By a visitation
That casts no shadow, a friend whose mild
Inquisitive glance lights with compassion,
Beyond the tomb, on all of this wild
And humbled creation.

It's hard to believe a spirit could die
Of such generous glow,
Or to doubt that somewhere a bird-sharp eye
Still broods on the capers of men below,
A stern voice asks the Immortals why
They should plague us so.

Dear poet, wherever you are, I greet you.
Much irony, wrong,
Innocence you'd find here to tease or entreat you,
And many the fate-fires have tempered strong,
But none that in ripeness of soul could meet you
Or magic of song.

Great brow, frail frame—gone. Yet you abide
In the shadow and sheen,
All the mellowing traits of a countryside
That nursed your tragi-comical scene;
And in us, warmer-hearted and brisker-eyed
Since you have been.

The Neurotic

The spring came round, and still he was not dead.
Skin of the earth deliciously powdered
With buttercups and daisies—oh, Proserpina
Refreshed by sleep, wild-cherry-garlanded
And laughing in the sallies of the willow-wren!
With lambs and lilies spring came round again.

Who would suppose, seeing him walk the meadows,
He walks a treadmill there, grinding himself
To powder, dust to greyer dust, or treads
An invisible causeway lipped by chuckling shadows?
Take his arm if you like, you'll not come near him.
His mouth is an ill-stitched wound opening: hear him.

'I will not lift mine eyes unto the hills
For there white lambs nuzzle and creep like maggots.
I will not breathe the lilies of the valley
For through their scent a chambered corpse exhales.
If a petal floats to earth, I am oppressed.
The grassblades twist, twist deep in my breast.'

The night came on, and he was still alive.
Lighted tanks of streets a-swarm with denizens
Darting to trysts, sauntering to parties.
How all the heart-fires twinkle! Yes, they thrive
In the large illusion of freedom, in love's net
Where even the murderer can act and the judge regret.

This man who turns a phrase and twiddles a glass
Seems far from that pale muttering magician

Pent in a vicious circle of dilemmas.
But could you lift his blue, thick gaze and pass
Behind, you would walk a stage where endlessly
Phantoms rehearse unactable tragedy.

'In free air captive, in full day benighted,
I am as one for ever out of his element
Transparently enwombed, who from a bathysphere
Observes, wistful, amazed, but more affrighted,
Gay fluent forms of life weaving around,
And dares not break the bubble and be drowned.'

His doomsdays crawled like lava, till at length
All impulse clogged, the last green lung consumed,
Each onward step required the sweat of nightmare,
Each human act a superhuman strength . . .
And the guillemot, clotted with oil, droops her head.
And the mouse between the elastic paws shams dead.

Death mask of a genius unborn:
Tragic prince of a rejected play:
Soul of suffering that bequeathed no myth:
A dark tower and a never-sounded horn.
Call him what we will, words cannot ennoble
This Atlas who fell down under a bubble.

The Misfit

At the training depot that first morning
When the west-country draft came forth on parade—
Mechanics, labourers, men of trade
Herded with shouts like boneheaded cattle—
One stood out from the maul
Who least of them all
Looked metal for killing or meat for the butchery blade.

He wore a long black cutaway coat
Which should have been walking by blackthorn-fleeced
Hedges to church; and good as a feast
Was the spare, wild face much weather had flavoured.
A shepherd or ploughman
I thought, or a cowman—
One with a velvet hand for all manner of beast.

I cannot forget how he stood, bemused,
With the meek eye of a driven thing:
But a solitude old as a cromlech ring
Was around him; a freeborn air of the downland,
A peace of deep combes
No world-anger consumes
Marked him off from the herd to be branded for soldiering.

I saw him not after. Is he now buried
Far from pastures buttercup-strewed,
Or tending his beasts again with the same rude

Rightness of instinct which then had brought him
So quaintly dressed
In his Sunday best
For the first step along the Calvary road?

From

AN ITALIAN VISIT

(1953)

A Letter from Rome

We have been here three days, and Rome is really—
I know, I know; it would take three life-times to cover
The glorious junk-heap. Besides, our generation—
Well, you've only to think of James, as one must do here,
Lapping the cream of antiquity, purring over
Each vista that stroked his senses, and in brief
Rubbing himself against Rome like a great tabby,
To see what I mean. We who 'flowered' in the Thirties
Were an odd lot; sceptical yet susceptible,
Dour though enthusiastic, horizon-addicts
And future-fans, terribly apt to ask what
Our all-very-fine sensations were in aid of.
We did not, you will remember, come to coo.
Still, there is hope for us. Rome has absorbed
Other barbarians: yes, and there's nobody quite so
Sensuously rich and reckless as the reformed
Puritan . . . This by the way, to establish a viewpoint.
        You wanted my impressions. If only one were
A simple sieve, be the mesh close or wide,
For Rome to shake (and how it does shake one!), sifting
Some finer stuff from the coarser. But the trouble with me is—
Or perhaps it's the trouble with Rome—to discrimate
Merely between what is here and what has been here,
Between the eye and the mind's eye. The place has had
Over two thousand years of advance publicity
For us, which clouds the taste and saps the judgment.
What are you to do when Catullus buttonholes you
On the way to St. Peter's? When the Colosseum presents

Nero* comparing notes with Roderick Hudson
On art and egotism? Sights, sounds, phantoms—
It is all too much for me, it should not be allowed!
　　　Perhaps, though, it is just here that something emerges.
As when, composing a poem, the tangle of images
And jangle of words pressing hard on you, mobbing you, may
Compel you to choose the right moment to disengage
And find the one word, the word of command which makes them
Meekly fall in to their ranks, and the march continues:
So from this Rome, where the past lies weltering
In the blood of the present, and posters of Betty Grable
Affront the ghost of Cato; from all its grandiose
Culs-de-sac—the monumental gateways
That open on nothing, the staircases starting for heaven,
The stone-blind palaces sweltering in the noon;
From the stilled tempest of the Sistine ceiling
To the water exasperated by sirocco
In every fountain basin; from the whole gamut,
Theatrical, vulgar, rhetorical, fractious, sublime,
Of a city young as Tithonus, a city so ancient
That even the shadows here lie thick as dust—
Emerges from all this, like invisible writing
Drawn out by the heart's warmth, one lucid word.
　　　Compost. I do not suppose the word original
(Original! Rome is quite beyond that). But think of it—
Century into century rotting down,
Faith piled on faith, Mithra on Jupiter,
Christ upon Mithra, Catholicism on Christ,
Temples imbedded in churches, church-stones in palaces:

　　* The Colosseum was built by Vespasian on the site of the Golden House
of Nero.

[86]

Think of the pagan gods, demoted to demons,
Haunting and taunting the Early Fathers; long-dead
Lights of love, immortalized as Madonnas,
Demurely smiling at man's infant idealism.
Superstition, sanctity, cruelty, laws, art, lust—
Layer after layer laid down, course upon course
They renew the soul of this city, a city whose prospects
Are quarried out of its bones, a soul digesting
All foreignness into one rich dark fibre.
Rome, I can tell you, is the very type of
The hugger-mugger of human growth. For here
You can see the grand design eternally crossed
By the abject means, and its seedy ruin redeemed with
Valerian, arbutus, fennel; a character root-fast
Like a man's in the deposit of all his acts.

     Or say, a woman's; for so she appeared to us
On the first morning when we sauntered out
(The night before, wild strawberries and Frascati
Gold as the Roman May-light, cool as grottoes).
A woman—how shall I put it?—who makes you feel
She has waited two thousand years to meet you, and now
At once she is wholly yours, her liquid tongue,
Her body mantled in the full flush of Ceres,
And Primavera fluttering in her eyes.
She can be tiresome, no doubt, feverish, languid,
Changing her moods like dresses. But today
She has chosen to be divinely acquiescent:
'What shall we do?' the shell-like murmur comes,
'Shall we go shopping? Would you like me to show you the sights?

I will do anything you say, anything.'
. . . So we took, in the end, a carrozza to St. Peter's.

The driver was plainly a phantom; his conveyance
Jarred like old bones and mumbled of better days when
Violet-adorned beauties, sedate or giddy,
Turned all heads on the Corso. Thus we went
Jaunting over the seven hills of Rome
With the streets rocking beneath us as if seven ages
Turned in their grave, while noise upon noise the drift
Of our own—its voices, horns, wheels, bells, loudspeakers—
Washed past us; then it dwindled away to a sea-shell
Cadence, beyond the Tiber, as we came near
Vatican city.

        And now *vates tacete*
Should be the word. Words here can only scrabble
Like insects at the plinth of a colossus,
Scrabble and feebly gesticulate and go elsewhere.
Mere magnitude one might deal with, or pure and simple
Meaning; but both in one, they give no purchase.
A dome superb as heaven's vault, capping a story
Whose hero blessed the meek; a desert of floor
Refracting faith like a mirage; the orchestration
Of gold and marble engulfing the still, small voice—
You cannot pass over St. Peter's and what it stands for,
Whether you see it as God's vicarious throne
Or the biggest bubble ever yet unpricked.
And here, I have to confess, the old Puritan peeped out;
Not in sour protest against the Scarlet Woman,
Nor quite in the mood of my generation—its volatile
Mixture of hero-worship and disrespect;
But that an early habit of going to church
Prevents me from going to churches, however distinguished
Their provenance, just as a sight-seer. Faith perhaps,
Though unconscious, is not yet dead, its breath still clouding

The glass of aesthetic perception. Apart from which,
I could not do with the guides who spring up like sweat-white
Fungi from every chink, and cling to one, furtively
Offering their curious knowledge; these pimps are not
The type you would choose to lead you to any altar.
So I was lost, ill at ease here, until by chance
In a side chapel we found a woman mourning
Her son: all the lacrimæ rerum flowed
To her gesture of grief, all life's blood from his stone.
There is no gap or discord between the divine
And the human in that pietà of Michelangelo.
Then, after a marathon walk through the Vatican galleries,
An endless belt of statues, tapestry, pictures
Glazing the eye, we came out into the streets again.
Better than all the museums, this strolling folk
Who sun themselves in the apricot light of antiquity
And take its prestige for granted. Cameo faces,
Contessa or contadina; bronze boys skylarking
As if they had just wriggled free from a sculptor's hand—
How easily art and nature overlap here!
Another thing you would like about the Romans
Is the way they use their city, not as a warren
Of bolt-holes, nor a machine into which one is fed
Each morning and at evening duly disgorged,
But as an open-air stage. Palazzo, tenement
Seem pure façade—back-cloth for a continuous
Performance of business, love-making, politics, idling,
Conducted with a grand operatic extravagance
At the tempo of family theatricals. That same night
In the Piazza del' Esedra, sipping
Grappa, we watched the people, warm as animals
And voluble as fountains, eddying round

While the floodlit masonry was mere slabs of moonshine.
Rome is a city where flesh and blood can never
Be sacrificed, or mistaken, for abstractions.

But already (you can imagine how) my mind's
Crisscrossed with figures, memoranda, lightning sketches,
Symbolic doodlings, hour by hour set down
Haphazardly as in Rome era on era.
And time is already shuffling tricks with discards.
Those fountains yesterday at the Villa d'Este
Grouped like patrician spectres in white conclave
Against a drop-scene of terraces and urns—
Did we indeed see them, or have they stepped
From a picture book years ago perused? Last night
We found on a wall of the Pincio a bas-relief,
A wide white calm imperious head suddenly
Surveying us out of the blank wall like some racial
Memory still not deep enough bricked up.

Yesterday, then, was a day with the dead. We hired
A car, and set out first for the Palatine hill.
The Forum? Well, picture a clearing found
In the depth of a clamorous forest, a low space littered
With bits of temples, arches, altars, mosaics
And God knows what—classical tags, fag ends,
Smatterings and stumps of a once apparently stable
Civilization, which packed up for all that
And left, like a gipsy encampment or picnic party:
And over it all, the silence of sheer exhaustion.
This area, sad as scar-tissue now, was the heart
Of a great republic, the S.P.Q.R.
Here they governed—a people, like the Scots,
Smouldering, pious, intolerant, living hard,
And demon fighters. Warlike was the seed;

But Time has pushed out this crop of decayed teeth.
It was the usual story. Long before
Their aqueducts ran dry and became picturesque,
Their virtue had imperceptibly seeped away
Into the dunes of ambition. They caught
Luxury, like a syphilis, from their conquests.
Then, feeling queer, they appointed one man to cure them
And made a god of him. The disease was arrested
From time to time. But injections grew more frequent,
And the extremities began to rot;
While at home no amount of marble could hide the sick core—
Vestals too free with their flame, tribunes long impotent,
A rabble who had not the wherewithal to redeem its
Too often pledged heirlooms, justice and hardiness.

    So we were glad on the whole to leave this spot
Where glum mementoes of decline and fall
Are cherished like a grievance in Rome's heart,
And drive out towards Tivoli. The name
Had a certain frivolous charm for one oppressed
By dwelling on ruined greatness. The little town,
Modishly perched on an olive-tressed hillside,
Is famous for its sulphur springs (our driver
Stopped the car so that we might inhale it)
And of course, for the Villa d'Este. There at first
In the elaborate Renaissance gardens
Laid out for the lust of the eye, you seem to see
The lineaments of gratified desire.
An illusion though, like the smile on a dead face
Which means nothing but our own wish for peace.
Exquisite, yes: but a sense of the past, to be truly
Felicitous, demands some belief in the present,
Some moral belvedere we have not got.

This villa inhabited only by frescoes,
This garden groomed for sightseers—they mirror
Too clearly our lack of prospect or tenable premise.
The cardinals and princes who adorned them,
Lords of an age when men believed in man,
Are as remote from us as the Colosseum
Where high-tiered beasts howled down professional heroes;
Perhaps—it is a comfortless thought—remoter.

      Back, then, to Rome. At Tivoli our driver
Stopped again like some house-proud, indelicate devil
To remark the smell of sulphur. Presently,
Held in a crook of Rome's old city wall
Close by St. Paul's gate under the pagan shadow
Of Gaius Cestius' pyramid, we found
The English cemetery. An ox-eyed, pregnant,
Slatternly girl opened the gate for us
And showed us round the desirable estate.
Here is one corner of a foreign field
That is for ever garden suburb. See,
In their detached and smug-lawned residences,
Behind a gauze of dusty shrubs, the English
Indulge their life-long taste for privacy.
Garish Campagna knocks at the back door,
Rome calls en grande tenue: but 'not at home'
Murmur these tombs, and 'far from home they died,
The eccentric couple you have come to visit—
One spitting blood, an outsider and a failure,
One sailing a boat, his mind on higher things.'
Somewhere close to the pyramid a loud-speaker
Blared jazz while we lingered at Keats' shabby mound,
But the air was drowned by the ghost of a nightingale;
The ground was swimming with anemone tears

Where Shelley lay.
                    We could feel at home here, with
This family of exiles. It is our people:
A people from whose reticent, stiff heart
Babble the springtime voices, always such voices
Bubbling out of their clay . . .
                    So much for Rome.
Tomorrow we shall take the bus to Florence.

Elegy Before Death: At Settignano

(*To R. N. L.*)

> . . . for be it never so derke
> Me thinketh I see hir ever mo.
> —CHAUCER

Come to the orangery. Sit down awhile.
The sun is setting: the veranda frames
An illuminated leaf of Italy.
Gold and green and blue, stroke upon stroke,
Seem to tell what nature and man could make of it
If only their marriage were made in heaven. But see,
Even as we hold the picture,
The colours are fading already, the lines collapsing
Fainting into the dream they will soon be.

Again? Again we are baffled who have sought
So long in a melting Now the formula
Of Always. There is no fast dye. Always?—
That is the word the sirens sing
On bone island. Oh stop your ears, and stop
All this vain peering through the haze,
The fortunate haze wherein we change and ripen,
And never mind for what. Let us even embrace
The shadows wheeling away our windfall days.

Again again again, the frogs are screeling
Down by the lilypond. Listen! I'll echo them—
Gain gain gain . . . Could we compel
One grain of one vanishing moment to deliver
Its golden ghost, loss would be gain

And Love step naked from illusion's shell.
Did we but dare to see it,
All things to us, you and I to each other,
Stand in this naked potency of farewell.

The villa was built for permanence. Man laid down
Like wine his heart, planted young trees, young pictures,
Young thoughts to ripen for an heir.
Look how these avenues take the long view
Of things ephemeral! With what aplomb
The statues greet us at the grassy stair!
Time on the sundial was a snail's migration
Over a world of warmth, and each day passing
Left on the fertile heart another layer.

The continuity they took for granted
We wistfully glamourize. So life's devalued:
Worth not a rhyme
These statues, groves, books, bibelots, masterpieces,
If we have used them only to grout a shaken
Confidence or stop up the gaps of time.
We must ride the flood, or go under
With all our works, to emerge, when it recedes,
Derelicts sluggish from the dishonouring slime.

Our sun is setting. Terrestrial planes shift
And slide towards dissolution, the terraced gardens
Quaver like waves, and in the garden urn
Geraniums go ashen. Now are we tempted, each
To yearn that his struggling counterpoint, carried away
Drowned by the flood's finale, shall return

To silence. Why do we trouble
A master theme with cadenzas
That ring out, fade out over its fathomless unconcern?

Love, more than our holidays are numbered.
Not one day but a whole life is drained off
Through this pinprick of doubt into the dark.
Rhadamanthine moment! Shall we be judged
Self-traitors? Now is a chance to make our flux
Stand and deliver its holy spark—
Now, when the tears rise and the levees crumble,
To tap the potency of farewell.
What ark is there but love? Let us embark.

A weeping firmanent, a sac of waters,
A passive chaos—time without wind or tide,
Where on brief motiveless eddy seethe
Lost faces, furniture, animals, oblivion's litter—
Envelop me, just as the incipient poem
Is globed in nescience, and beneath
A heart purged of all but memory, grows.
No landfall yet? No rift in the film? . . . I send you
My dove into the future, to your death.

*   *   *

A dove went forth: flits back a ghost to me,
Image of her I imagine lost to me,
Up the road through Fiesole we first travelled on—
Was it a week or thirty years ago?
Time vanishes now like a mirage of water,
Touched by her feet returning whence she had gone,
Touched by the tones that darkly appeal to me,

The memories that make her shade as real to me
As all the millions breathing under the upright sun.

We are back at the first time we went abroad together.
Homing to this garden with a love-sure bent
Her phantom has come. Now hand in hand we stray
Through a long-ago morning mounting from a lather
Of azaleas and dizzy with the lemon blossom's scent.
And I seem to hear her murmur in the old romantic way,
'So blissfully, rosily our twin hearts burn here,
This vernal time, whenever we return here,
To haunter and haunted will be but yesterday.'

I follow her wraith down the terraced gardens
Through a dawn of nightingales, a murmurous siesta,
By leaf-green frogs on lily leaves screeling again
Towards eve. Is it dark or light? Fireflies glister
Across my noon, and nightlong the cicadas
Whir like a mechanical arm scratching in the brain.
All yesterday's children who fleetingly caressed her
Break ranks, break time, once more to join and part us:
I alone, who possessed her, feel the drag of time's harsh chain.

'Ah, you,' she whispers; 'are you still harping
On mortal delusion? still the too much hoping
Who needs only plant an acorn to dream a dryad's kiss?
Still the doubtful one who, when she came to you
Out of the rough rind, a naked flame for you,
Fancied some knot or flaw in love, something amiss?'
Yes, such I am. But since I have found her
A revenant so fleshed in my memories, I wonder
Is she the real one and am I a wisp from the abyss.

Dare I fellow her through the wood of obscurity—
This ilex grove where shades are lost in shade?
Not a gleam here, nothing differs, nothing sings, nothing grows,
For the trees are columns which ebonly support
A crypt of hollow silence, a subliminal thought,
A theorem proving the maggot equivalent to the rose.
Undiminished she moves here, shines, and will not fade.
Death, what had she to do with your futile purity,
The dogma of bone that on rare and common you would impose?

Her orbit clasped and enhanced in its diadem
All creatures. Once on a living night
When cypresses jetted like fountains of wine-warm air
Bubbling with fireflies, we going outside
In the palpitating dark to admire them,
One of the fireflies pinned itself to her hair;
And its throbbings, I thought, had a tenderer light
As if some glimmering of love inspired them,
As if her luminous heart was beating there.

Ah, could I make you see this subtle ghost of mine,
Delicate as a whorled shell that whispers to the tide,
Moving with a wavering watersilk grace,
Anemone-fingered, coral-tinted, under whose crystalline
Calm such naiads, angel fish and monsters sleep or slide;
If you could see her as she flows to me apace
Through waves through walls through time's fine mesh magically
                                                        drawn,
You would say, this was surely the last daughter of the foam-born,
One whom no age to come will ever replace.

Eve's last fainting rose cloud; mornings that restored her

With orange tree, lemon tree, lotus, bougainvillea:
The milk-white snake uncoiling and the flute's light-fingered
                                           charm:
Breast of consolation, tongue of tried acquaintance:
A tranquil mien, but under it the nervous marauder
Slithering from covert, a catspaw from a calm:
Heaven's city adored in the palm of a pictured saint:
My vision's *ara coeli*, my lust's familiar,
All hours, moods, shapes, desires that yield, elude, disarm—

All woman she was. Brutalizing, humanizing,
Pure flame, lewd earth was she, imperative as air
And weak as water, yes all women to me.
To the rest, one of many, though they felt how she was rare
In sympathy and tasted in her warm words a sweetness
Of life that has ripened on the sunny side of the tree.
To herself a darker story, as she called her past to witness—
A heart much bruised, how often, how stormily surmising
Some chasmal flaw divided it from whole felicity.

So I bless the villa on the hill above Fiesole,
For here and now was flawless, and the past could not encroach
On its charmed circle to menace or to taunt her.
Oh, time that clung round her in unfading drapery,
Oh, land she wore like an enamelled brooch,
It was for remembrance you thus adorned her!
Now as I look back, how vividly, how gracefully
Ghosting there, she breathes me not the ghost of a reproach.
Happiness, it seems, can be the best haunter.

You later ones, should you see that wraith divulged for a moment
Through the sleep-haze of plumbago, glancing out from the loggia's

Vain dream of permanence as from a page
Time is already turning again, will you thus comment?—
'She is some dead beauty, no doubt, who queened here awhile
And clasped her bouquets, and shrinks to leave the lighted stage:
Not quite of the villa's classic period, though—
Something more wistful, ironic, unstable in act and style,
A minor masterpiece of a silver age.'

But to me she stands out tall as the Torcello madonna
Against a mosaic of sunlight, for ever upholding
My small, redeeming love, But 'love is all,'
She says; and the mortal scene of planets and tides,
Animals, grass and men is transformed, proved, steadied around me.
But her I begin to view through a thickening veil,
A gauze of tears, till the figure inscrutably fades—
As every vision must vanish, if we and it keep faith,
Into the racked, unappeasable flesh of the real.

*   *   *

But look, the garden storm is stilled, the flood
Blinked away like a tear, earth reconciled to
Her molten birth-bed's long prophetic throes!
Her hills are lizards in their solid trance
Of sun and stone: upon each hill
Vine and olive hold the archaic pose:
Below, the bubble dome looks everlasting
As heaven's womb, and threading the eyes of bridges
Arno endlessly into the loom of oblivion flows.

A ghost, the mere thought of a shade, has done it.
Testing the shifty face of the Now with a dove, I found

Terra firma. Whatever in me was born to praise
Life's heart of blood or stone here reached its zenith,
Conjuring, staying, measuring all by that meek shade . . .
Now, love, you have tried on your phantom dress,
Return to nakedness!
Be breathing again beside me, real, imperfect!
Enmesh, enact my dream till it vanishes!

The oranges are going out? Tomorrow
Will light them up again. Tomorrow will call you
With nightingales; tomorrow will leave
A rose by your plate, and freshen the plumbago's
Blue millinery and open a parasol
Of cedar for you, as it did for the first, ignorant Eve
Before exile or death was thought of. But we know well
On what tenure we have this garden. Each day's a livelier
Paradise when each dawn is a reprieve.

I imagine you really gone for ever. Clocks stop.
Clouds bleed. Flames numb. My world shrunk to an echoing
Memorial skull. (A child playing at hide-
And-seek suddenly feels the whole terrible truth of Absence.)
Too keen the imagined grief, too dearly gained
Its proof of love. I would let all else slide,
Dissolve and perish into the old enigma,
If that could keep you here, if it could keep
Even your sad ghost at my side.

But gold and green and blue still glows before us
This leaf of Italy, the colours fixed,
The characters formed by love. It is love's way
To shine most through the slow dusk of adieu.

[101]

Long may it glow within us, that timeless, halcyon halt
On our rough journey back to clay.
Oh, may my farewell word, may this your elegy
Written in life blood from a condemned heart
Be quick and haunting even beyond our day.

From

PEGASUS AND OTHER POEMS

(1957)

Almost Human

The man you know, assured and kind,
Wearing fame like an old tweed suit—
You would not think he has an incurable
Sickness upon his mind.

Finely that tongue, for the listening people,
Articulates love, enlivens clay;
While under his valued skin there crawls
An outlaw and a cripple.

Unenviable the renown he bears
When all's awry within? But a soul
Divinely sick may be immunized
From the scourge of common cares.

A woman weeps, a friend's betrayed,
Civilization plays with fire—
His grief or guilt is easily purged
In a rush of words to the head.

The newly dead, and their waxwork faces
With the look of things that could never have lived,
He'll use to prime his cold, strange heart
And prompt the immortal phrases.

Before you condemn this eminent freak
As an outrage upon mankind,
Reflect: something there is in him
That must for ever seek

To share the condition it glorifies,
To shed the skin that keeps it apart,
To bury its grace in a human bed—
And it walks on knives, on knives.

An Episode

So then he walled her up alive
(It seemed that her betrayal must deserve
What his own agony felt like—the slow choking
Of breath and pore in a close grave)
And waited. There was no cry from her, no knocking.

—Waited for pain to end, with her
Who had been his love and any comer's whore.
Soft-spoken dreams revealed how he was wanting
The victim to turn comforter—
A chastened ghost, an unreproachful haunting.

Presently the blank wall grew eyes
That haunted him from every covert ease
And thickset pain. He felt as if heart were searching
For heart. He saw in those whitewashed eyes
A look neither forgiving nor beseeching.

His bloody fingers tore at the wall,
Demolishing what could never salve nor seal
Its crime, but found in the nook where he had placed her
No twisted limbs, no trace at all.
His heart lay there—a mess of stone and plaster.

Sheepdog Trials in Hyde Park

A shepherd stands at one end of the arena.
Five sheep are unpenned at the other. His dog runs out
In a curve to behind them, fetches them straight to the shepherd,
Then drives the flock round a triangular course
Through a couple of gates and back to his master: two
Must be sorted there from the flock, then all five penned.
Gathering, driving away, shedding and penning
Are the plain words for the miraculous game.

An abstract game. What can the sheepdog make of such
Simplified terrain?—no hills, dales, bogs, walls, tracks,
Only a quarter-mile plain of grass, dumb crowds
Like crowds on hoardings around it, and behind them
Traffic or mounds of lovers and children playing.
Well, the dog is no landscape-fancier: his whole concern
Is with his master's whistle, and of course
With the flock—sheep are sheep anywhere for him.

The sheep are the chanciest element. Why, for instance,
Go through this gate when there's on either side of it
No wall or hedge but huge and viable space?
Why not eat the grass instead of being pushed around it?
Like a blob of quicksilver on a tilting board
The flock erratically runs, dithers, breaks up,
Is reassembled: their ruling idea is the dog;
And behind the dog, though they know it not yet, is a shepherd.

The shepherd knows that time is of the essence
But haste calamitous. Between dog and sheep

There is always an ideal distance, a perfect angle;
But these are constantly varying, so the man
Should anticipate each move through the dog, his medium.
The shepherd is the brain behind the dog's brain,
But his control of dog, like dog's of sheep,
Is never absolute—that's the beauty of it.

For beautiful it is. The guided missiles,
The black-and-white angels follow each quirk and jink of
The evasive sheep, play grandmother's-steps behind them,
Freeze to the ground, or leap to head off a straggler
Almost before it knows that it wants to stray,
As if radar-controlled. But they are not machines—
You can feel them feeling mastery, doubt, chagrin:
Machines don't frolic when their job is done.

What's needfully done in the solitude of sheep-runs—
Those rough, real tasks become this stylised game,
A demonstration of intuitive wit
Kept natural by the saving grace of error.
To lift, to fetch, to drive, to shed, to pen
Are acts I recognise, with all they mean
Of shepherding the unruly, for a kind of
Controlled woolgathering is my work too.

Final Instructions

For sacrifice, there are certain principles—
Few, but essential.

I do not mean your ritual. This you have learnt—
The garland, the salt, a correct use of the knife,
And what to do with the blood:
Though it is worth reminding you that no two
Sacrifices ever turn out alike—
Not where this god is concerned.

The celebrant's approach may be summed up
In three words—patience, joy,
Disinterestedness, Remember, you do not sacrifice
For your own glory or peace of mind:
You are there to assist the clients and please the god.

It goes without saying
That only the best is good enough for the god.
But the best—I must emphasize it—even your best
Will by no means always be found acceptable.
Do not be discouraged:
Some lizard or passing cat may taste your sacrifice
And bless the god: it will not be entirely wasted.

But the crucial point is this:
You are called only to make the sacrifice:
Whether or no he enters into it
Is the god's affair; and whatever the handbooks say,
You can neither command his presence nor explain it—

All you can do is to make it possible.
If the sacrifice catches fire of its own accord
On the altar, well and good. But do not
Flatter yourself that discipline and devotion
Have wrought the miracle: they have only allowed it.

So luck is all I can wish you, or need wish you.
And every time you prepare to lay yourself
On the altar and offer again what you have to offer,
Remember, my son,
Those words—patience, joy, disinterestedness.

Lot 96

Lot 96: a brass-rimmed ironwork fender.
It had stood guard for years, where it used to belong,
Over the hearth of a couple who loved tenderly.
Now it will go for a song.

Night upon winter night, as she gossiped with him
Or was silent, he watched the talkative firelight send
Its reflections twittering over that burnished rim
Like a language of world without end.

Death, which unclasped their hearts, dismantled all.
The world they made is as if it had never been true—
That firelit bubble of warmth, serene, magical,
Ageless in form and hue.

Now there stands, dulled in an auction room,
This iron thing—a far too durable irony,
Reflecting never a ghost of the lives that illumed it,
No hint of the sacred fire.

This lot was part of their precious bond, almost
A property of its meaning. Here, in the litter
Washed up by death, values are re-assessed
At a nod from the highest bidder.

Moods of Love

1

The melting poles, the tongues that play at lightning,
All that gross hurricane hatched from a sigh—
These are the climax to his sure routine.
But first, a glance coins gold in the air, doves issue
From clasped hands, knots no one saw tied are tightening;
The card you chose, or were made to, wondrously
Turns up here there and anywhere like a djinn,
And borrowed time vanishes to amaze you.

Admire the 'fluence of this conjuring
As once again he runs the gamut through
Of tricks you can neither fathom nor resist,
Though well you know the old Illusionist
Employs for his whole repertoire only two
Simple properties—a rod, a ring.

2

Think of his transformations; thirsty babe,
Secret companion, devil, confidante,
Lapdog and sphinx—each hides that king whose orb
Is the whole earth grasped in a bare 'I want.'
Redder the rose for him, sadder the fall,
Who swells a trivial word into a portent,
Turns dust to diamond, shows the bantam tall,
The giant weak: nevertheless, most potent
When he comes back insidious and subdued
As an old jailbird begging one more chance.

Making trite things unique—you reckon it
Tells more than brute necessity at play?

Unwise. Another tedious, piteous woman
Was Helen, got by heart. Can you adore
The human animal's ecstacy, yet ignore
The ground and primitive logic of being human?—

Deplore that closest viewed is clearliest changing,
And least enduring is the most enthralling?
That love breeds habit, habit brings estranging?
That highest flown means most abysmal falling?

When the flushed hour goes down, what residue
From its broad-glittering flood remains to you?

7

Shells, weed, discoloured wrack—a spring tide's litter
Dully recalling its lost element,
And one you live with, quarrelsome or complying,
Are all that's left of Aphrodite's birth.
Gone is the power she gave you to delight her,
The period of grace, so quickly spent,
When the day's walk was a white dream of flying,
Earth a far cry, she a sufficient earth.

Whether long use has now choked your desire
With its own clinker, or, abruptly parted
At love's high noon, incredulous you have stood
Suffering her absence like a loss of blood

Week after week, still, by the god deserted,
You worship relics of a sacred fire.

8

Beware! Such idolizing can divorce
Body and mind: the foam-bright fiction drains
Purpose away and sings you from your course.
Better a brutal twitching of the reins
And off, than this devouring pious whore
Who in a soft regret will twine you fast
Where thigh-bones mope along the tainted shore
And crazed beachcombers pick over their past.
Love is the venturing on: think—as you fare
Among strange islands, each a phantasy
Of home, giving your strength to what must be
Found and new-found through doubt, mirage, despair—
Weaving, unweaving her true self somewhere
Deep in your heart grows a Penelope.

9

If love means exploration—the divine
Growth of a new discoverer first conceived
In flesh, only the stranger can be loved:
Familiar loving grooves its own decline.

If change alone is true—the ever-shifting
Base of each real or illusive show,
Inconstancy's a law: the you that now
Loves her, to otherness is blindly drifting.

But chance and fretting time and your love change her
Subtly from year to year, from known to new:
So she will always be the elusive stranger,
If you can hold her present self in view.

Find here, in constant change, faithful perceiving,
The paradox and mode of all true loving.

The House Where I Was Born

An elegant, shabby, white-washed house
With a slate roof. Two rows
Of tall sash windows. Below the porch, at the foot of
The steps, my father, posed
In his pony trap and round clerical hat.
This is all the photograph shows.

No one is left alive to tell me
In which of those rooms I was born,
Or what my mother could see, looking out one April
Morning, her agony done,
Or if there were pigeons to answer my cooings
From that tree to the left of the lawn.

Elegant house, how well you speak
For the one who fathered me there,
With your sanguine face, your moody provincial charm,
And that Anglo-Irish air
Of living beyond one's means to keep up
An era beyond repair.

Reticent house in the far Queen's County,
How much you leave unsaid.
Not a ghost of a hint appears at your placid windows
That she, so youthfully wed,
Who bore me, would move elsewhere very soon
And in four years be dead.

I know that we left you before my seedling

Memory could root and twine
Within you. Perhaps that is why so often I gaze
At your picture, and try to divine
Through it the buried treasure, the lost life—
Reclaim what was yours, and mine.

I put up the curtains for them again
And light a fire in their grate:
I bring the young father and mother to lean above me,
Ignorant, loving, complete:
I ask the questions I never could ask them
Until it was too late.

Time to Go

The day they had to go
Was brilliant after rain. Persimmons glowed
In the garden behind the castle.
Upon its wall lizards immutably basked
Like vitrified remains
Of an archaic, molten summer. Bronze
Cherubs shook down the chestnuts
From trees over a jetty, where fishing nets
Were sunshine hung out in skeins
To dry, and the fishing boats in their little harbour
Lay breathing asleep. Far
And free, the sun was writing, rewriting ceaselessly
Hieroglyphs on the lake—
Copying a million, million times one sacred
Vanishing word, peace.
The globed hours bloomed. It was grape-harvest season,

And time to go. They turned and hurried away
With never a look behind,
As if they were sure perfection could only stay
Perfect now in the mind,
And a backward glance would tarnish or quite devalue
That innocent, golden scene.
Though their hearts shrank, as if not till now they knew
It was paradise where they had been,
They broke from the circle of bliss, the sunlit haven.
Was it for guilt they fled?
From enchantment? Or was it simply that they were driven
By the migrant's punctual need?

All these, but more—the demand felicity makes
For release from its own charmed sphere,
To be carried into the world of flaws and heartaches,
Reborn, though mortally, there.

So, then, they went, cherishing their brief vision.
One watcher smiled to see
Them go, and sheathed a flaming sword, his mission
A pure formality.

From

REQUIEM FOR THE LIVING

(1955)

The Room

FOR GEORGE SEFERIS

To this room—it was somewhere at the palace's
Heart, but no one, not even visiting royalty
Or reigning mistress, ever had been inside it—
To this room he'd retire.
Graciously giving himself to, guarding himself from
Courtier, suppliant, stiff ambassador,
Supple assassin, into this unviewed room
He, with the air of one urgently called from
High affairs to some yet loftier duty,
Dismissing them all, withdrew.

And we imagined it suitably fitted out
For communing with a God, for meditation
On the Just City; or, at the least, a bower of
Superior orgies . . . He
Alone could know the room as windowless
Though airy, bare yet filled with the junk you find
In any child-loved attic; and how he went there
Simply to taste himself, to be reassured
That under the royal action and abstraction
He lived in, he was real.

The Disabused

(a Dramatic Monologue)

Eleven o'clock. My house creaks and settles,
Feeling the dry-rot in its old bones. Well,
It will see me out; and after that, who cares?
More than a house is perishing—civilization,
For all I know; and Helen's marriage, she tells me,
Breaking up—a mishap she seems to confuse
With the end of the world, poor girl. 'You are so calm,
You amaze me, father,' she said: 'I feel I cannot
Keep my head above water any longer.'
Now she has taken her tragedy to bed.
But what storms first!—this indelicate need of woman
To have emotion—hers, his, anyone's exposed
Like bleeding lumps of meat on a butcher's counter
And poke at it with insensitive, finicky fingers!
'Helen,' I might have said, 'if I am calm
It is because I have spent most of a lifetime
Learning to live with myself, which is the hardest
Marriage of all.' But to say this would only
Have underlined her notion that I had somehow
Failed her. The way she spoke about my calmness
Was to reproach me, of course, for having failed—
Not in recognizing what she suffers,
But in refusing to be infected by it:
For that's what women want—that we vibrate
To their disturbance, visibly respond—
Tears, smiles, exasperation, pity, rage,
Any response will satisfy them, for so

Their weakness sees its power. She'll never grasp
How a man grows strong by silently outstaring
His brute infirmity. 'Helen,' I all but told her,
'Tomorrow is the fortieth anniversary
Of the day I let my brother drown.'

                                    Not 'saw'
Or 'watched'—you notice, Tom—but 'let.' I never
Permit myself the soft and venial option . . .
It's the first morning of a summer holiday
After the War. You are just demobbed, and I,
Three years younger, finished with school. We run
Along the cliff path—harebell, scabious, rampion,
Sunlight and dew on the grass—and we are running
Back into the boyhood of our world.
You, always the leader, stand at the waves' edge
Undressed, before I have scrambled down the steep path
Among those yellow poppies to the beach.
Then, like a new slide thrown on the screen, with a click
The picture is different—I on the shingle, you
Thirty yards out suddenly thrashing the calm sea
To foam, as if you had been harpooned. This happens
So quickly, and yet your dying seems to go on
For ever. You struggle silently, your eyes
Howling for help. And I, a feeble swimmer,
Must let you drown or flounder out and let you
Drag me under.

                    But there was no choice, really:
Fear, like an automatic governor,
Shut off the power in my limbs, held me down
So hard that a flint dug my bare sole open
(I have the stigma now). The cove contained
My tiny shouts. My eyes searched everywhere—

Foreshore and cliff and heaven—at first for help,
But soon to make sure there was no witness of
Your dying and my living, or perhaps
Most of all to avoid your whitening stare.
No one in sight; and at last the sea's face too
Was empty. Now I could look. Along the horizon,
Slow as a minute hand, there faintly moved
A little ship, a model of indifference.
So it went.
                    You have omitted one thing.
No, Tom, I was coming to that. I lay down
In the shallows to saturate my clothes.
('What presence of mind,' you say? A coward soon
Learns circumspection.) So, when I got home
Crying, limping, dripping with brine, father
In his crammed anguish still found room to praise me,
Console and praise me for having done my best.

There's this to be said for growing old—one loses
The itch for wholeness, the need to justify
One's maimed condition. I have lived all these years
A leper beneath the skin, scrupulous always
To keep away from where I could spread contagion.
No one has guessed my secret. I had to learn
Good and early the know-how of consuming
My own waste products: I at least have never
Contaminated soil or river. Why,
Why then, though I have played the man in facing
My worst, and cauterized the ugly wound,
Does that original morning by the sea
Still irk me like a lovers' tryst unkept—
Not with remorse or tragedy curses—no,

With the nostalgic sweetness of some vision
All but made flesh, then vanishing, which drains
Colour and pith from the whole aftertime?
I lost a brother

     Only a brother?

       Tom,
Do you mean self-respect? We have had this out
A hundred times. You know I have regained it,
Stiffening my heart against its primal fault.
'There was the fault,' you say? What? Do you blame
The wound for the scar-tissue, or a bombed site
For growing willowherb? It is nature's way.
You who gulped the sea and are dead, why do you
Keep swimming back with these cast-off things in your mouth
Like an imbecile dog?

     The vision. The sweet vision.
Recapture. A last chance.

       This is beyond me!
Last chance of what? Is it your elder-brotherly
Pleasure to keep me wallowing in that sour
Humiliation? You can teach me nothing
About the anatomy of fear—I've made it
A life-long study, through self-vivisection:
And if I did use local anaesthetics
To deaden the area, better a witness than
A victim to the science of self knowledge.
Relentlessly I have tracked each twist and shuffle,
Face-saving mask, false candour, truth-trimmed fraud,
All stratagems of bluster and evasion—
Traced them back along the quivering nerves
To that soft monster throned in my being's chasm,
Till I was armed in and against the infirmity.

[129]

And there's my hand reaching out to take it.
Reaching! Alive! . . .

                              My God, I needed that.
What a grotesque hallucination! Really,
I could have sworn my arm was paralysed
For a few moments. If I were superstitious,
I'd say it was a sign from heaven—yes, Tom,
It rather proves my point—a sign that I
Was right not to embroil myself in Helen's
Hysterical maelstrom. What she needs from me
Is rational guidance, realism, detachment,
Not facile gestures of pure self-indulgence.
You and your 'vision,' Tom! No, I'm not buying it.
One delusion is quite enough . . . I'd better
Ring MacIntyre in the morning, and arrange
For him to give me a thorough overhaul.

Circus Lion

Lumbering haunches, pussyfoot tread, a pride of
Lions under the arcs
Walk in, leap up, sit pedestalled there and glum
As a row of Dickensian clerks.

Their eyes are slag. Only a muscle flickering,
A bored, theatrical roar
Witness now to the furnaces that drove them
Exultant along the spoor.

In preyward, elastic leap they are sent through paper
Hoops at another's will
And a whip's crack: afterwards, in their cages,
They tear the provided kill.

Caught young, can this public animal ever dream of
Stars, distances and thunders?
Does he twitch in sleep for ticks, dried water-holes,
Rogue elephants, or hunters?

Sawdust, not burning desert, is the ground
Of his to-fro, to-fro pacing,
Barred with the zebra shadows that imply
Sun's free wheel, man's coercing.

See this abdicated beast, once king
Of them all, nibble his claws:
Not anger enough left—no, nor despair—
To break his teeth on the bars.

This Young Girl

This young girl, whose secret life
Vagues her eyes to the reflective, lucent
Look of the sky topping a distant
Down beyond which, invisible, lies the sea—

What does she mark, to remember, of the close things
That pearl-calm gaze now shines upon? . . .
Her mother, opening a parasol,
Drifts over the hailed-with-daisies lawn:

Head full of designs, her father
Is pinned to drawing board: two brothers settle
For cool jazz in the barn: a little
Sister decides to become Queen Pocahontas.

Or is it the skyline viewed from her attic window
Intimating the sea, the sea
Which far off waits? or the water garden
Fluent with leaves and rivulets near by,

That will be her memory's leitmotif?
All seems acceptable—an old house sweetened
By wood-ash, a whole family seasoned
In dear pursuits and country gentleness.

But her eyes elude, this summer's day. Far, far
Ahead or deep within they peer,
Beyond those customary things
Towards some Golden Age, that is now, is here.

Walking Away

FOR SEAN

It is eighteen years ago, almost to the day—
A sunny day with the leaves just turning,
The touch-lines new-ruled—since I watched you play
Your first game of football, then, like a satellite
Wrenched from its orbit, go drifting away

Behind a scatter of boys. I can see
You walking away from me towards the school
With the pathos of a half-fledged thing set free
Into a wilderness, the gait of one
Who finds no path where the path should be.

That hesitant figure, eddying away
Like a winged seed loosened from its parent stem,
Has something I never quite grasp to convey
About nature's give-and-take—the small, the scorching
Ordeals which fire one's irresolute clay.

I have had worse partings, but none that so
Gnaws at my mind. Perhaps it is roughly
Saying what God alone could perfectly show—
How selfhood begins with a walking away,
And love is proved in the letting go.

Elegy for a Woman Unknown

(F. P.)

1

At her charmed height of summer—
Prospects, children rosy,
In the heart's changeful music
Discords near resolved—
Her own flesh turned upon her:
The gross feeder slowly
Settled to consume her.

Pain speaks, bearing witness
Of rank cells that spawn
To bring their temple down.
Against such inmost treachery
Futile our protesting:
The body creates its own
Justice and unjustness.

Three times flesh was lopped,
As trees to make firebreak
(In their natural flowering
Beautiful the trees):
Three times her enemy leapt
The gap. Three years of dying
Before the heart stopped.

Upon the shrinking islands
Of flesh and hope, among
Bitter waves that plunged,

Withdrew to lunge yet deeper,
Patient, unreconciled,
She wrote poems and flung them
To the approaching silence.

Upon the stretching hours
Crucified alone,
She grew white as a stone
Image of endurance;
Soft only to the cares
Of loved ones—all concern
For lives that would soon lack hers.

Dying, did she pass through
Despair to the absolute
Self-possession—the lightness
Of knowing a world indifferent
To all we suffer and do,
Shedding the clung-to load
Of habit, illusion, duty?

You who watched, phase by phase,
Her going whose life was meshed
With yours in grief and passion,
Remember now the unspoken,
Unyielding word she says—
How, in ruinous flesh,
Heroic the heart can blaze.

2

Island of stone and silence. A rough ridge
Chastens the innocent azure. Lizards hang

Like their own shadows crucified on stone
(But the heart palpitates, the ruins itch
With memories amid the sunburnt grass). Here sang
Apollo's choir, the sea their unloosed zone.
Island of stillness and white stone.

Marble and stone—the ground-plan is suggested
By low walls, plinths, lopped columns of stoa, streets
Clotted with flowers dead in June, where stood
The holy place. At dusk they are invested
With Apollonian calm and a ghost of his zenith heats.
But now there are no temples and no god:
Vacantly stone and marble brood,

And silence. Not the silence after music,
But the silence of no more music. A breeze twitches
The grass like a whisper of snakes; and swallows there are,
Cicadas, frogs in the cistern. But elusive
Their chorusing—thin threads of utterance, vanishing stitches
Upon the gape of silence, whose deep core
Is the stone lions' soundless roar.

Lions of Delos, roaring in abstract rage
Below the god's hill, near his lake of swans!
Tense haunches, rooted paws set in defiance
Of time and all intruders, each grave image
Was sentinel and countersign of deity once.
Now they have nothing to keep but the pure silence.
Crude as a schoolchild's sketch of lions,

They hold a rhythmic truth, a streamlined pose.
Weathered by sea-winds into beasts of the sea,

Fluent from far, unflawed; but the jaws are toothless,
Granulated by time the skin, seen close,
And limbs disjointed. Nevertheless, what majesty
Their bearing shows—how well they bear these ruthless
Erosions of their primitive truth!

Thyme and salt on my tongue, I commune with
Those archetypes of patience, and with them praise
What in each frantic age can most incline
To reverence; accept from them perfection's myth—
One who warms, clarifies, inspires, and flays.
Sweetness he gives but also, being divine,
Dry bitterness of salt and thyme.

The setting sun has turned Apollo's hill
To darker honey. Boulders and burnt grass.
A lyre-thin wind. A landscape monochrome.
Birds, lizards, lion shapes are all stone-still.
Ruins and mysteries in the favouring dusk amass,
While I reach out through silence and through stone
To her whose sun has set, the unknown.

3

We did not choose to voyage.
Over the ship's course we had little say,
And less over the ship. Tackle
Fraying; a little seamanly skill picked up on our way;
Cargo, that sooner or later we should
Jettison to keep afloat for one more day.
But to have missed the voyage—

That would be worse than the gales, inglorious calms,
Hard tack and quarrels below. . . .
Ship's bells, punctual as hunger; dawdling stars;
Duties—to scrub the deck, to stow
Provisions, break out a sail: if crisis found us of one mind,
It was routine that made us so,
And hailed each landfall like a first-born son.

Figure to yourself the moment
When, after weeks of the crowding emptiness of sea
(Though no two waves are the same to an expert
Helmsman's eye), the wind bears tenderly
From an island still invisible
The smell of earth—of thyme, grass, olive tree:
Fragrance of a woman lost, returning.

And you open the bay, like an oyster, but sure there'll be
A pearl inside; and rowing ashore,
Are received like gods. They shake down mulberries into
Your lap, bring goat's cheese, pour
Fresh water for you, and wine. Love too is given.
It's for the voyaging that you store
Such memories; yet each island seems your abiding-place.

. . . For the voyaging, I say.
And not to relieve its hardships, but to merge
Into its element. Bays we knew
Where still, clear water dreamed like a demiurge
And we were part of his fathomless dream;
Times, we went free and frisking with dolphins through the surge
Upon our weather bow.

Those were our best hours—the mind disconnected
From pulsing Time, and purified
Of accidents: those, and licking the salt-stiff lips,
The rope-seared palms, happy to ride
With sea-room after days of clawing from off a lee shore,
After a storm had died.
Oh, we had much to thank Poseidon for.

Whither or why we voyaged,
Who knows? . . . A worst storm blew. I was afraid.
The ship broke up. I swam till I
Could swim no more. My loves and memories are laid
In the unrevealing deep . . . But tell them
They need not pity me. Tell them I was glad
Not to have missed the voyage.

The Dam

It mounted up behind his cowardice
And self-regard. Fearing she would expose
His leper tissue of half-truths and lies
When, hurt, she probed at him, he tried to gloze
That fear as patience with her sick mistrust
Of him: he could not answer her appeal,
Nor recognise how his was the accursed
Patience of flesh that can no longer feel. . . .
Love had once mounted up behind his fear
Of being exposed in love's whole helplessness,
And broke it down, and carried him to her
On the pure, toppling rage for nakedness . . .
A spate of her reproaches. The dam broke.
In deluging anger his self-hatred spoke.

Ideal Home

1

Never would there be lives enough for all
The comely places—
Glimpsed from a car, a train, or loitered past—
That lift their faces
To be admired, murmuring 'Live with me.'

House with a well,
Or a ghost; by a stream; on a hill; in a hollow: breathing
Woodsmoke appeal,
Fresh paint, or simply a prayer to be kept warm,
Each casts her spell.

Life, claims each, will look different from my windows,
Your furniture be
Transformed in these rooms, your chaos sorted out here.
Ask for the key.
Walk in, and take me. Then you shall live again.

2

. . . Nor lives enough
For all the fair ones, dark ones, chestnut-haired ones
Promising love—
I'll be your roof, your hearth, your paradise orchard
And treasure-trove.

With puritan scents—rosemary, thyme, verbena,
With midnight musk,

Or the plaintive, memoried sweetness tobacco-plants
Exhale at dusk,
They lure the footloose traveller to dream of

One fixed demesne,
The stay-at-home to look for his true self elsewhere.
I will remain
Your real, your ideal property. Possess me.
Be born again.

3

If only there could be lives enough, you're wishing? . . .
For one or two
Of all the possible loves a dozen lifetimes
Would hardly do:
Oak learns to be oak through a rooted discipline.

Such desirableness
Of place or person is chiefly a glamour cast by
Your unsuccess
In growing yourself. Rebirth means more than a change of
Flesh or address.

Switch love, move house—you will soon be back where you started,
On the same ground,
With a replica of the old romantic phantom
That will confound
Your need for roots with a craving to be unrooted.

From

THE ROOM

(1965)

The Way In

The right way in would be hard to find—
Not for want of a door, but because there were so many,
Each commanding a different kind
Of approach, and then committing him to
An unretraceable step. If he faced
The flunkey's sneer and the snarling wolfhounds,
He would soon discover that getting past
Them was the least of his troubles. He lacked
The hero's invincible charm: to go
Without card of introduction or book
Of etiquette was bad; but worse, he had no
Ground-plan given him for what would be
Less of a mansion, he feared, than a maze.
Still, through state apartments and ancestor-lined
Passages, beyond a door of green baize,
He knew there must be that innermost room
Where She, alone, waited. Waited for whom?

No doubt she was at home. He had seen her mooning
Around the garden—pearl feet, gold crown
Proved her a princess—early every morning
In the ghostfall dew by the dreaming cedars.
No sentry, mastiff or chains could he spy,
But he felt her a captive . . . Now, crawling through
The grass of the lawn, which had grown head-high
Since he came, he listened at a gloomed french window
Faint sounds he heard: they might have been
Cries for help or his own voice calling
From sleep. Ventured a glance: obscene

Slug trails and spider webs pasted the glass.
Frantic to peel away the cataract spell
He circled the domicile, trying each door:
Bells, knockers, handles—he tried them all.
But all in a repudiating hush was locked;
Till a window opened, a wide mouth mocked.

So he went home, romantic even in disgrace,
And told his father the whole sad story.
Who said: 'To be sure, I remember the place,
And the afternoon I felt like going there.
I walked through the door—there is only one,
By the way—and yes, I remember a crown
Of tawny hair. I tumbled it down.
She sighed for relief. I took her, bare
And crowing as a babe, on the kitchen floor.'

Derelict

for A. D. Peters

The soil, flinty at best, grew sour. Its yield
Receding left the old farm high and dry
On a ledge of the hills. Disused, the rutted field-
Track fades, like the sound of footsteps, into a sigh
For any feet to approach this padlocked door.
The walls are stained and cracked, the roof's all rafter.
We have come where silence opens to devour
Owl-cry, wind-cry, all human memories . . . After
So many working life-times a farm settles
For leisure, and in the tenth of a life-time goes
To seed . . . A harrow rusts among harsh nettles.
She who in love or protest grew that rose
Beneath her window, left nothing else behind
But a mangle in the wash-house. The rose now
Looks mostly thorn and sucker; the window's blind
With cobwebs. Dilapidated!—even the low
Front wall is ragged: neighbours have filched its stone
To build their pigsties, maybe; but what neighbours?—
Never did a farm stand more alone.
Was it the loneliness, then, and not their labour's
Poor yield that drove them out? A farmer's used
To the silence of things growing, weather breeding.
More solitude, more acres. He'd be amused
To hear it's human company he was needing,
With a wife to bake, wash, mend, to nag or share
The after-supper silence, children to swing
From those rheumatic apple trees; and where

The docks run wild, his chained-up mongrel barking
If anyone climbed a mile off on the hill.
He'd not abandon cheerfully a place
In which he'd sunk his capital of skill
And sweat. But if earth dies on you, it's no disgrace
To pull up roots . . . Now, all that was the farm's—
The same demands of seasons, the plain grit
And homely triumph—deepens and informs
The silence you can hear. Reverence it.

Saint Anthony's Shirt

> We are like the relict garments of a Saint: the same and not the same: for the careful Monks patch it and patch it: till there's not a thread of the original garment left, and still they show it for St. Anthony's shirt.
>
> KEATS: *Letter to Reynolds*

This moving house of mine—how could I care
If, wasting and renewing cell by cell,
It's the ninth house I now have tenanted?
I cannot see what keeps it in repair
Nor charge the workmen who, its changes tell,
Build and demolish it over my head.

Ninth house and first, the same yet not the same—
Are there, beneath new brickwork, altering style,
Viewless foundations steady through the years?
Hardly could I distinguish what I am
But for the talkative sight-seers who file
Through me, the window-view that clouds or clears.

The acting, speaking, lusting, suffering I
Must be a function of this house, or else
Its master principle. Is I a sole
Tenant created, recreated by
What he inhabits, or a force which tells
The incoherent fabric it is whole?

If master, where's the master-thread runs through
This patchwork, piecemeal self? If occupant
Merely, the puppet of a quarrelsome clique,

How comes the sense of selfhood as a clue
Embodying yet transcending gene and gland?
The I, though multiple, is still unique.

I walk these many rooms, wishing to trace
My frayed identity. In each, a ghost
Looks up and claims me for his long-lost brother—
Each unfamiliar, though he wears my face.
A draught of memory whispers I was most
Purely myself when I became another:

Tending a sick child, groping my way into
A woman's heart, lost in a poem, a cause,
I touched the marrow of my being, unbared
Through self-oblivion. Nothing remains so true
As the outgoingness. This moving house
Is home, and my home, only when it's shared.

Fishguard to Rosslare

From all my childhood voyages back to Ireland
Only two things remembered: gulls afloat
Off Fishguard quay, littering a patch of radiance
Shed by the midnight boat.

And at dawn a low, dun coast shaping to meet me,
An oyster sky opening above Rosslare . . .
I rub the sleep from my eyes. Gulls pace the moving
Mast-head. We're almost there.

Gulls white as a dream on the pitch of Fishguard harbour,
Paper cut-outs, birds on a lacquered screen;
The low coastline and the pearl sky of Ireland;
A long sleep in between.

A sleep between two waking dreams—the haven,
The landfall—is how it appears now. The child's eye,
Unpuzzled, saw plain facts: I catch a glint from
The darkness they're haunted by.

Pietà

Naked, he sags across her cumbered knees,
Heavy and beautiful like the child she once
Aroused from sleep, to fall asleep on the next breath.

The passion is done,
But death has not yet stiffened him against her,
Nor chilled the stripling grace into a dogma.
For a timeless hour, imagined out of marble,
He comes back to his mother, he is all
And only hers.

And it is she whom death has magnified
To bear the burden of his flesh—the arms
Excruciated no more, the gash wiped clean.
A divine, dazed compassion calms her features.
She holds all earth's dead sons upon her lap.

*   *   *

In the triumphal car
Closely escorted through the gaze and heart of
A city, at the height of his golden heyday,
He suddenly slumps.

Cameras show her bending to shelter him
(But death has moved faster), and then a pink
Nimbus veiling the exploded skull.

No order here, no artistry, except for
The well-drilled wounds, the accomplished sacrifice.
But from that wreck

Two living images are saved—the wife who
Nurses a shattered world in her lap;

And, flying the coffin home, refuses to change
Out of her yellow, blood-spattered dress, with
'Let them all see what was done to him.'

For Rex Warner on His Sixtieth Birthday

'The hawk-faced man'—thirty-five years ago
I called him—'who could praise an apple
In terms of peach and win the argument' . . .
Oxford between the wars. I at the age of dissent
From received ideas, admiring a man so able
At undermining the crusted status quo.

But he was no sophist, this unsophisticated
Son of a Modernist clergyman, who came down
From a Cotswold height with the larks of Amberley
And the lays of Catullus running wild in his head. We,
Two green youths, met by chance in a Jacobean
Quad. From that term our friendship's dated.

Friendship, I'd guess, has not much more to do
With like minds, shared needs, than with rent or profit:
Nor is it the love which burns to be absolute, then dies
By inches of ill-stitched wounds, of compromise:
But a kind of grace—take it or leave it.
'Keeping up' a friendship means it is through.

That grace I accept. When he returns at last
From Egypt, Greece, the States, we take up where
We left. Right friendships are that homing, each to the other,
On frequencies unchanged through time or weather.
And still, though bulkier, he'll appear
In focus with the young self I knew first—

Scholar, wing three-quarter, and bird-watcher:
Self-contained, yet an affable bar-crony:

A mind of Attic dash and clarity,
Homeric simpleness, and natural charity
For all but intellectual cliques and their baloney—
So was he then. And since, each new departure

Proved him, though wayward, all of a piece.
Working a spell of allegoric art,
In *The Wild Goose Chase* and *The Aerodrome*
He formed a style intrinsic, dry and firm—
Revetment against the chaos in his and a nation's heart—
As, centuries ago, Thucydides.

Fable or fact, living and dead, he carries
Greece near his heart. Rocks, olives, temples, sea and sun
In lucid paradigm express
His tonic scepticism, cordial address.
Pericles and Prometheus spoke through one
Loved by Sikelianós and great Seferis.

Enough that in a pretentious age, when all—
Love, politics, art, right down to money—is cheapened,
He'll take each issue for what it's worth, not wincing,
Inflating, prancing his ego there, romancing
A tragic fall: if deaths have happened
In him, through him, he never preached at the funeral.

It's friendship we return to in the end:
Past selves are kept alive in it, a living
Communion flows from their dead languages. A home
Enlarged by absences, mellowed by custom,
Undemanding, simply taking and giving,
Is he, our sixty-year-old friend.

My Mother's Sister

I see her against the pearl sky of Dublin
Before the turn of the century, a young woman
With all those brothers and sisters, green eyes, hair
She could sit on; for high life, a meandering sermon

(Church of Ireland) each Sunday, window-shopping
In Dawson Street, picnics at Killiney and Howth . . .
To know so little about the growing of one
Who was angel and maid-of-all-work to my growth!

—Who, her sister dying, took on the four-year
Child, and the chance that now she would never make
A child of her own; who, mothering me, flowered in
The clover-soft authority of the meek.

Who, exiled, gossiping home chat from abroad
In roundhand letters to a drift of relations—
Squires', Goldsmiths, Overends, Williams'—sang the songs
Of Zion in a strange land. Hers the patience

Of one who made no claims, but simply loved
Because that was her nature, and loving so
Asked no more than to be repaid in kind.
If she was not a saint, I do not know

What saints are . . . Buying penny toys at Christmas
(The most a small purse could afford) to send her
Nephews and nieces, she'd never have thought the shop
Could shine for me one day in Bethlehem splendour.

Exiled again after ten years, my father
Remarrying, she faced the bitter test
Of charity—to abdicate in love's name
From love's contentful duties. A distressed

Gentle woman housekeeping for strangers;
Later, companion to a droll recluse
Clergyman brother in rough-pastured Wexford,
She lived for all she was worth—to be of use.

She bottled plums, she visited parishioners.
A plain habit of innocence, a faith
Mildly forbearing, made her one of those
Who, we were promised, shall inherit the earth.

. . . Now, sunk in one small room of a Rathmines
Old people's home, helpless, beyond speech
Or movement, yearly deeper she declines
To imbecility—my last link with childhood.

The battery's almost done: yet if I press
The button hard—some private joke in boyhood
I teased her with—there comes upon her face
A glowing of the old, enchanted smile.

So, still alive, she rots. A heart of granite
Would melt at this unmeaning sequel. Lord,
How can this be justified, how can it
Be justified?

On Not Saying Everything

This tree outside my window here,
Naked, umbrageous, fresh or sere,
Has neither chance nor will to be
Anything but a linden tree,
Even if its branches grew to span
The continent; for nature's plan
Insists that infinite extension
Shall create no new dimension.
From the first snuggling of the seed
In earth, a branchy form's decreed.

Unwritten poems loom as if
They'd cover the whole of earthly life.
But each one, growing, learns to trim its
Impulse and meaning to the limits
Roughed out by me, then modified
In its own truth's expanding light.
A poem, settling to its form,
Finds there's no jailer, but a norm
Of conduct, and a fitting sphere
Which stops it wandering everywhere.

As for you, my love, it's harder,
Though neither prisoner nor warder,
Not to desire you both: for love
Illudes us we can lightly move
Into a new dimension, where
The bounds of being disappear
And we make one impassioned cell.

So wanting to be all in all
Each for each, a man and woman
Defy the limits of what's human.

Your glancing eye, your animal tongue,
Your hands that flew to mine and clung
Like birds on bough, with innocence
Masking those young experiments
Of flesh, persuaded me that nature
Formed us each other's god and creature.
Play out then, as it should be played,
The sweet illusion that has made
An eldorado of your hair
And our love an everywhere.

But when we cease to play explorers
And become settlers, clear before us
Lies the next need—to re-define
The boundary between yours and mine;
Else, one stays prisoner, one goes free.
Each to his own identity
Grown back, shall prove our love's expression
Purer for this limitation.
Love's essence, like a poem's, shall spring
From the not saying everything.